AF609491

POEMS & DRAWINGS
FROM LOVE, LIFE, AND NATURE

volume two

A THOUSAND PEBBLES SING

Richard Knight

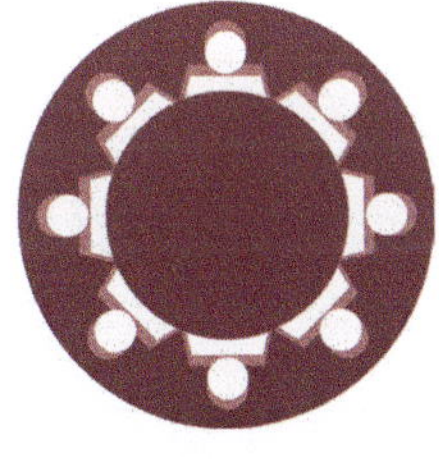

Cross Roads Publications

ISBN 978-0-9524392-5-7

Printed and bound in the United States of America. Typeset in Bliss.

The author's thanks and appreciation go to Ian Shoobridge for the design and layout of this publication, Paul Phillips, IT Consultant for technical advice and guidance, Steve Ellefsen, from Vivado Marketing Communications for his support, and Andrew McCulloch for proof reading of the final draft.

Poems and Drawings from Love, Life, and Nature
Volume Two
A Thousand Pebbles Sing

Published by:
Cross Roads Publications, 16 South Primrose Hill, Chelmsford, Essex, CM1 2RG, UK
t. 07966174466

CONTENTS

TO THE READER

This is a book to dip into as and when your mood or need takes you. It's content acknowledges that emotional growth is about being aware of the possibility of a deeper and more meaningful contact with the world around us, and with our inner world of beliefs, feelings, and values, creating for us a greater sense of 'oneness', and inner-harmony.

Sketching and drawing directly from nature, like writing about how events and moments affect us, can establish that special unity. By simply observing through the direct path of seeing and contemplation, a source of renewal and self-discovery can be found. It is by fully engaging with our daily experience of life that a more rewarding sense of who we are, or who we may become, will evolve!

The poems and drawings were all inspired by a momentary sensation or passing event, for example: a scene, an object, a smile, a new insight, the faint scent of snowdrops, sunlight upon a crystal.

Each poem is to be read as a separate entity, standing by itself, and not part of a sequence. The reflective rather than speculative aim of many of the poems implies an emotional record.

You will see that the poems are built around a regular syllabic structure. Each poem consists of twenty-two syllables arranged line by line as five, five, seven, and five. The aim being to trap a moment's vision or experience into the net of twenty-two syllables. The very nature of poetry is about saying much with few words and the meaning of some poems will only expand as our experience expands. The more we can give to them the more they can give to us.

The comments beneath the drawings are primarily from my field notes, and are a way of introducing the drawings to you. The drawings will, I trust, like the poems, speak to you for themselves, and in their own language.

My hope is that you will discover something of value here, if only for a moment, in your life's journey of self-discovery, enjoyment, and an awakening presence.

My thanks,

Richard

Chelmsford City

2012

POEMS & DRAWINGS
FROM LOVE, LIFE, AND NATURE

volume two

A THOUSAND PEBBLES SING

1

The fifteenth of May

Meditations gift

Old foundations are shaken

Fire and water born.

2

Glowing suntan face

Upon pure white silk

Soft snow covers the hillside

The full moon resting.

3

Framing a picture

Of hop-fields in Kent

Departing swallows circle

The evening sky.

Early Morning Mist

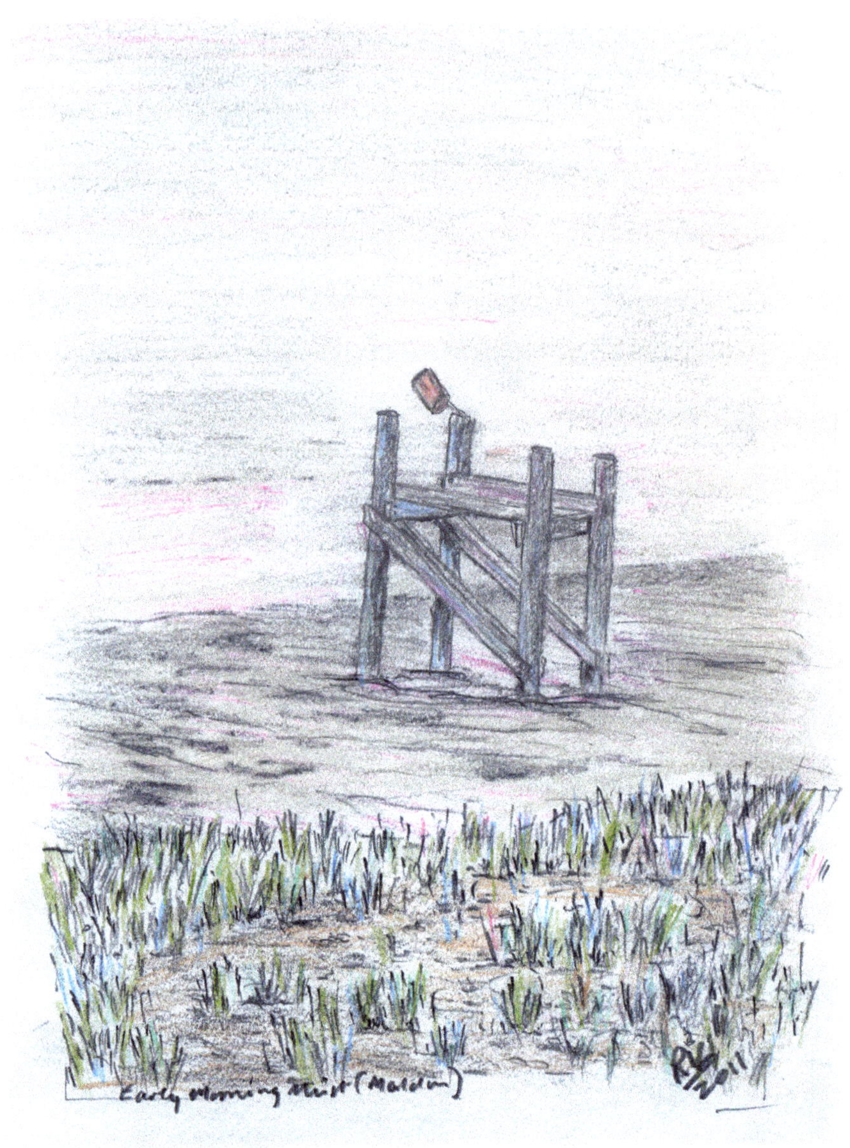

Whilst enjoying the estuary at Maldon I thought of the once-upon-a-time vast Essex marshes and wetlands, fog and dripping mists, jellied eels and pickled herrings. The red tin reminded me of a flag waving at a passing sail barge. The promenade is still, its history hidden in the mist, on this Sunday morning.

4

Her right hand held high

Waves again farewell

Then turning I see a flag

Flying at half-mast.

Built in 1797

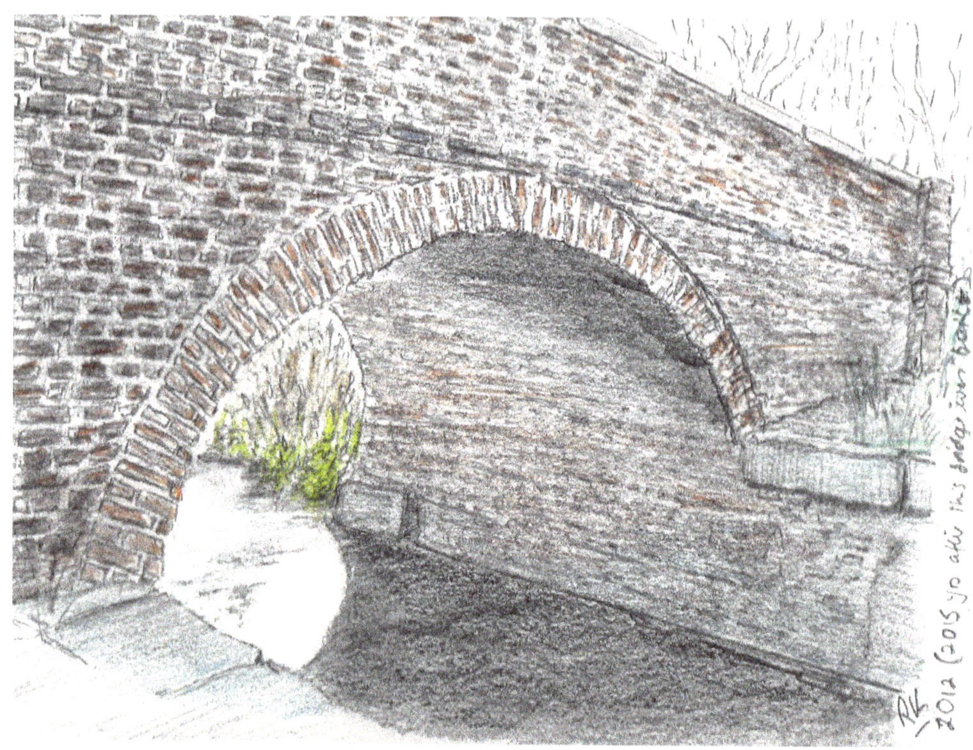

This beautiful bridge goes across the last canal to be built in England, before the railways arrived. Drawn, facing downstream, soft red bricks, secrets and warmth, beside the old lock in Springfield basin, Chelmsford, on a beautiful springtime morning. See from the reflection, the sun is already moving toward the south. I enjoyed catching the curve of that reflection, best viewed as a message I thought! That inevitable passing of the day!

Railway Viaduct

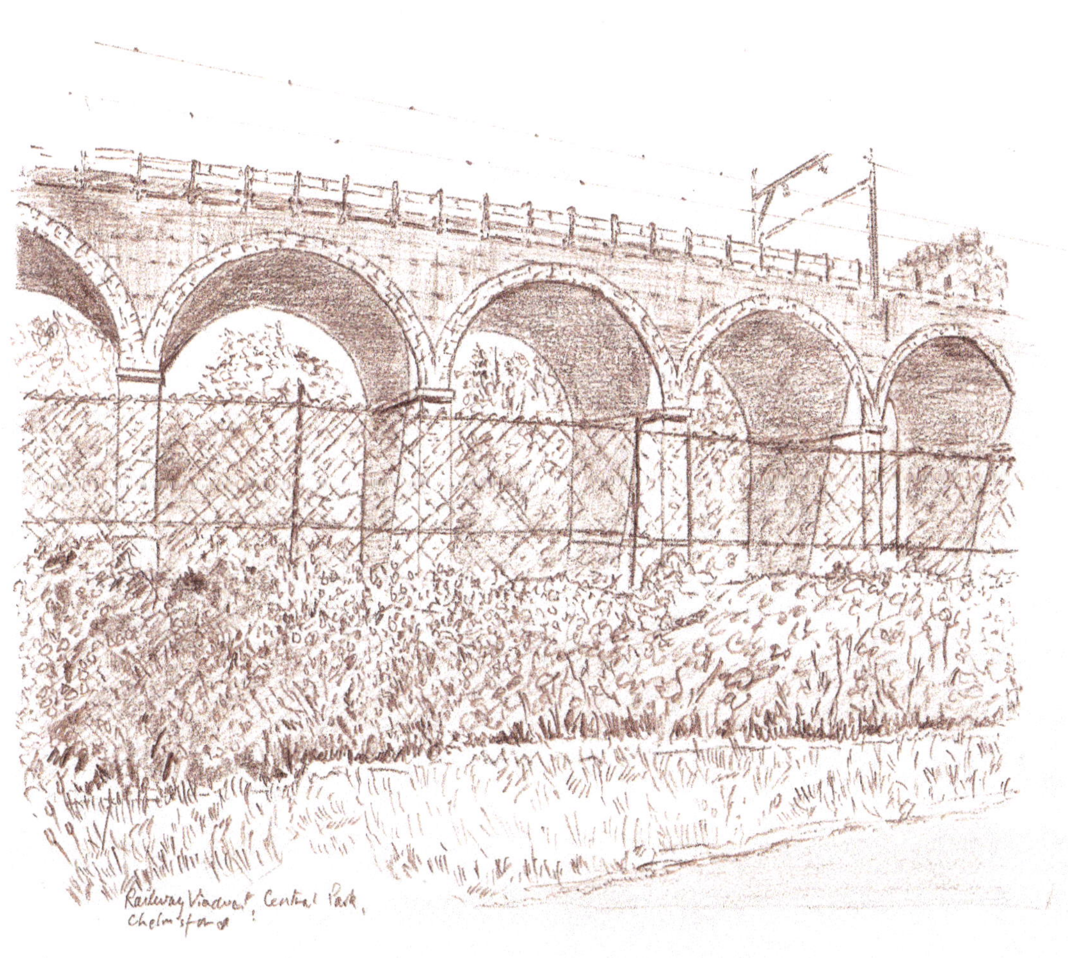

This railway viaduct (18 arches in all) was built in 1842. What structures they are! Symmetry, proportion, harmony, scale. A tribute to the age of steam, to those who built them, and still used daily by thousands of commuters. (The lake in Central Park, Chelmsford, is the result of tons of earth being dug out in order to form an embankment further along from these actual arches drawn here, towards the station.)

5

With a joyful heart

Watching sparrows play

Wood-ember sparks dart freely

As twilight falls.

6

A single hinge

Holds the barn door

The strain of disharmony

Threatens existence.

Near Kelvedon, Essex

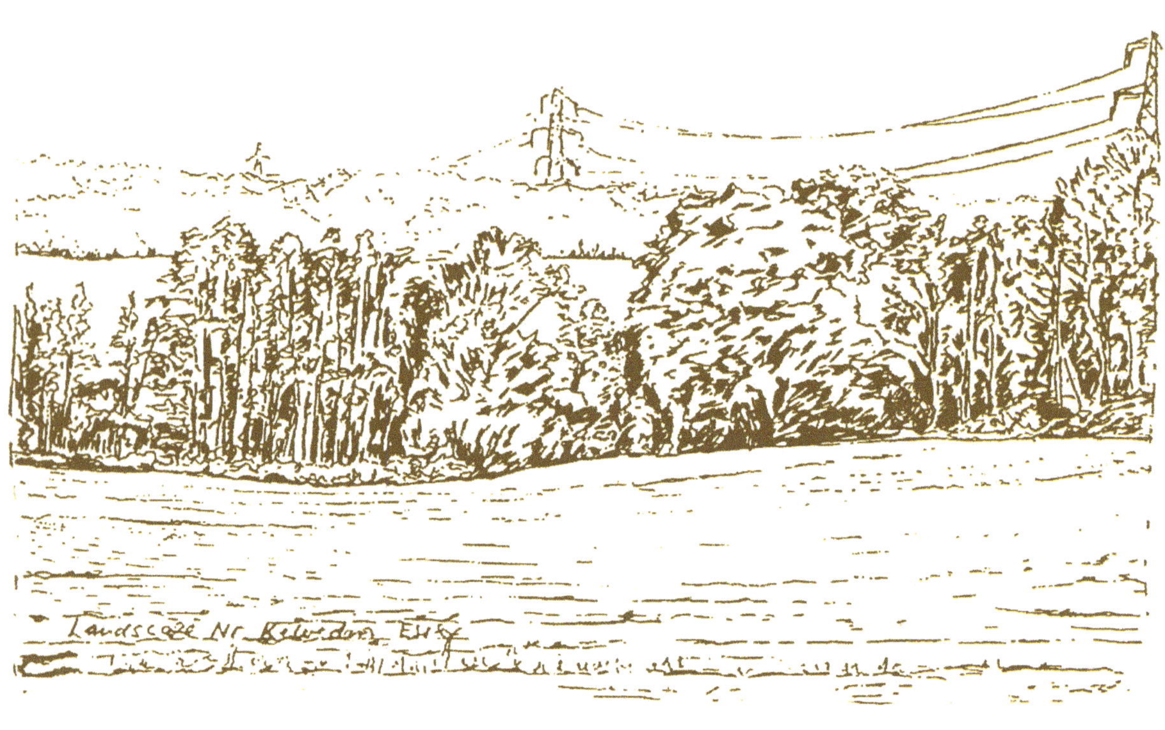

I moved from London to Essex in 1970 and discovered the beauty and pleasure of the Essex countryside. Sketched from the roadside, the pylons marching across these open fields, the trees and hedges appeared to reflect a glorious indifference to this advance of progress... having seen it many times before!

7

Ploughed umber land

Raw sienna sky

Auburn hair gently rolling

Over bare shoulders.

Chevrolet (Imperial War Museum)

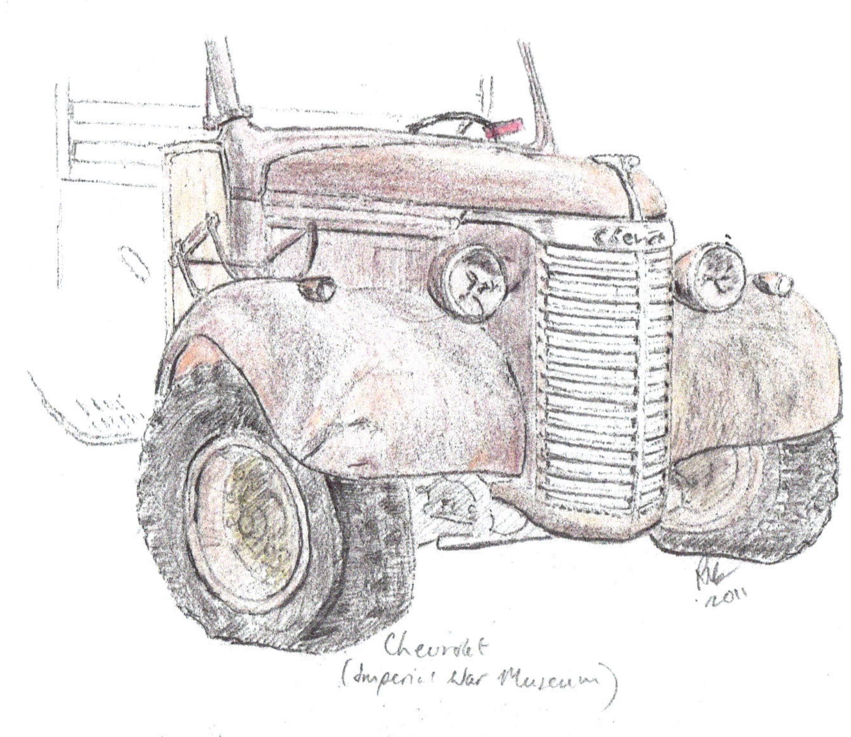

Such an evocative subject, asking to be drawn. Reminded me of 1950s America whose culture was such an influence upon me. The blues, rock n' roll, and the effects of a war that still disturbs the hearts and lives of many. Lest we forget.

My First Car

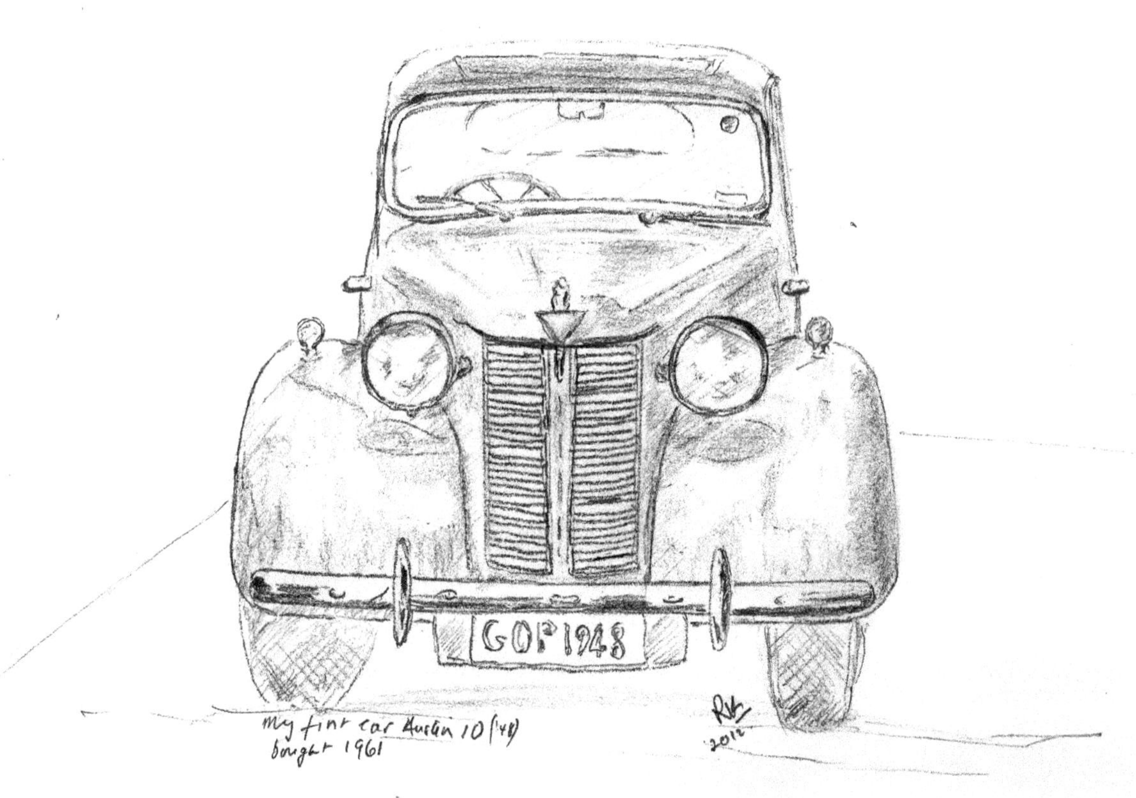

1961, £50 down with £35 on the book (hire purchase), the open road at 55 mph top speed, first family holiday, Norfolk. Freedom, transport cafes, juke boxes, and growing up.

8

Like a horse tethered

To a painted rail

I am tied to attachment

There is no freedom.

Essex Sail Barges, Maldon

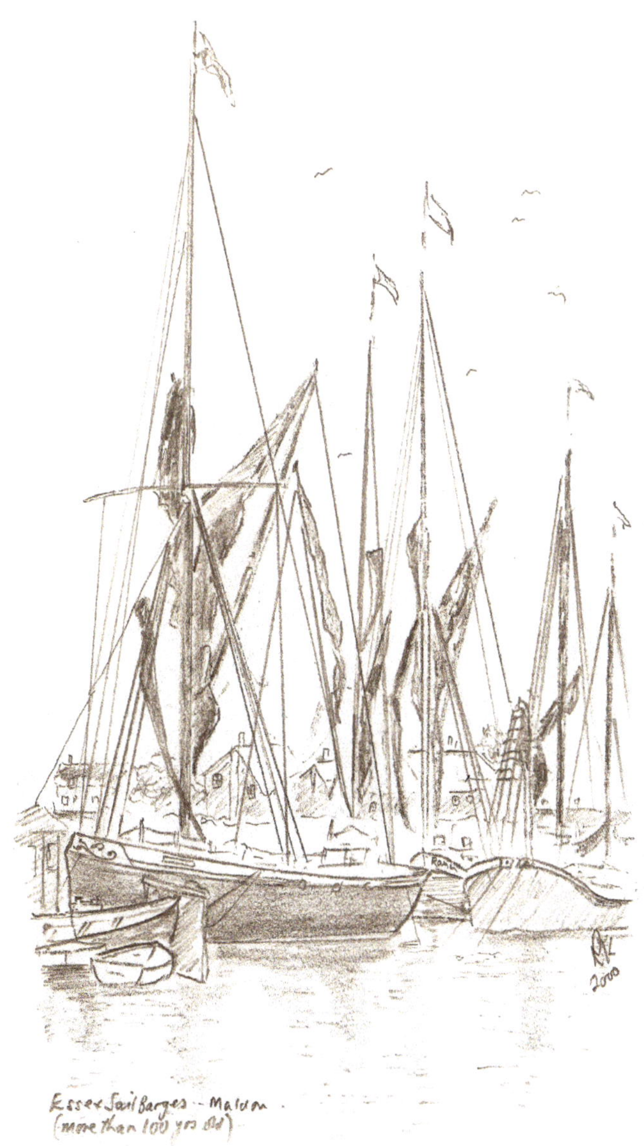

These vessels are over 100 years old. The last survivors of a fleet that brought trade to the Essex coast and old London Town. A captain plus one deck-hand could work these boats. Impressed by their elegance, rested sails, and high mast. I sensed a continuous 'undercurrent' of nostalgia and resistance. Such beautiful shapes against the sky.

9

Crossing the dark ford

Sadness in my heart

December clouds sinking

Behind barren trees.

10

Warm morning sunshine

Blessing our bedroom

Daffodils in the kitchen

Celebrating Spring.

In the Dark

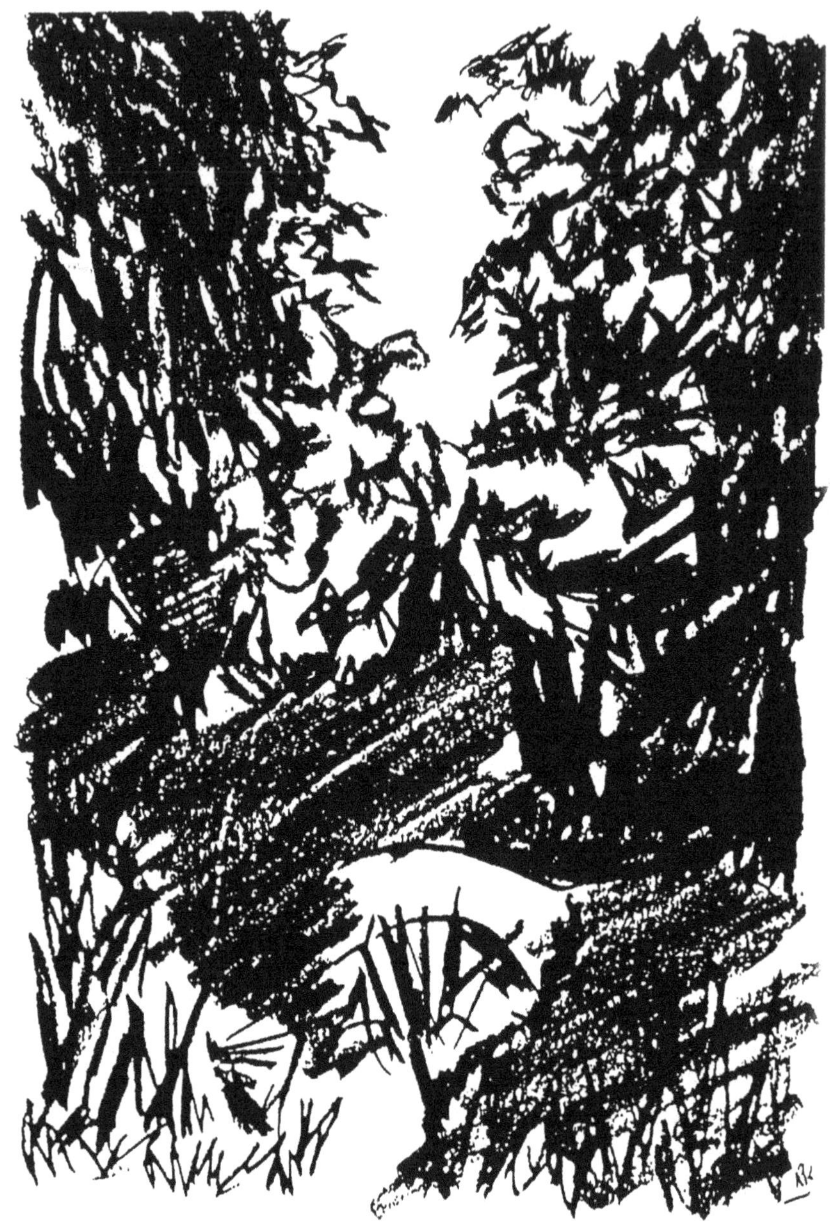

With this Conte-crayon sketch I tried to evoke a wood-block image in order to embrace the creaking and cracking sound of the trees on this dark, cold night, in Bedfordshire. (The little brick-bridge, otherwise lost in the undergrowth, crossed a stagnant muddy stream, surrendering, almost forgotten).

11

Stella Blue fallen

Creating darkness

Everything is nothing

Lost without moonlight.

12

Eating together

From the same clear bowl

Feeling a true harmony

Breathing the same air.

Walking to Guadamar

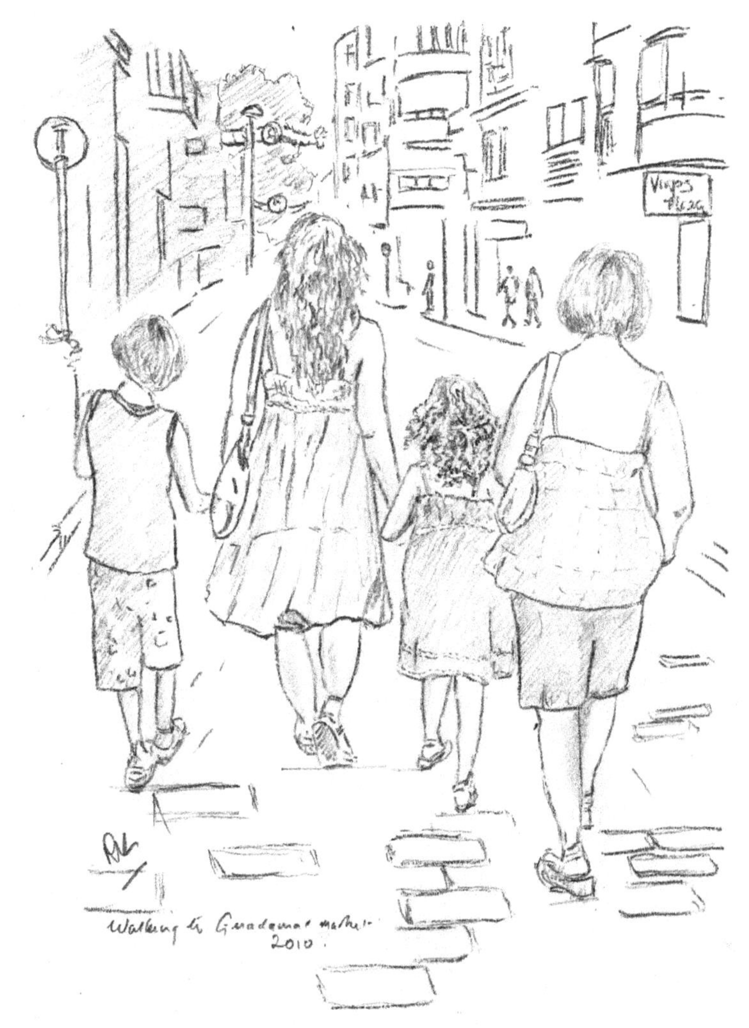

A most precious family, together in Spain, knowing for once their direction – the market place by the Mediterranean Sea

13

Yes I said goodbye

Thinking you would know

How I wish to be with thee

Say once more hello.

14

Laughing together

By a wishing well

Listen to the coin answer

Nothing is for free.

Pampas Grass

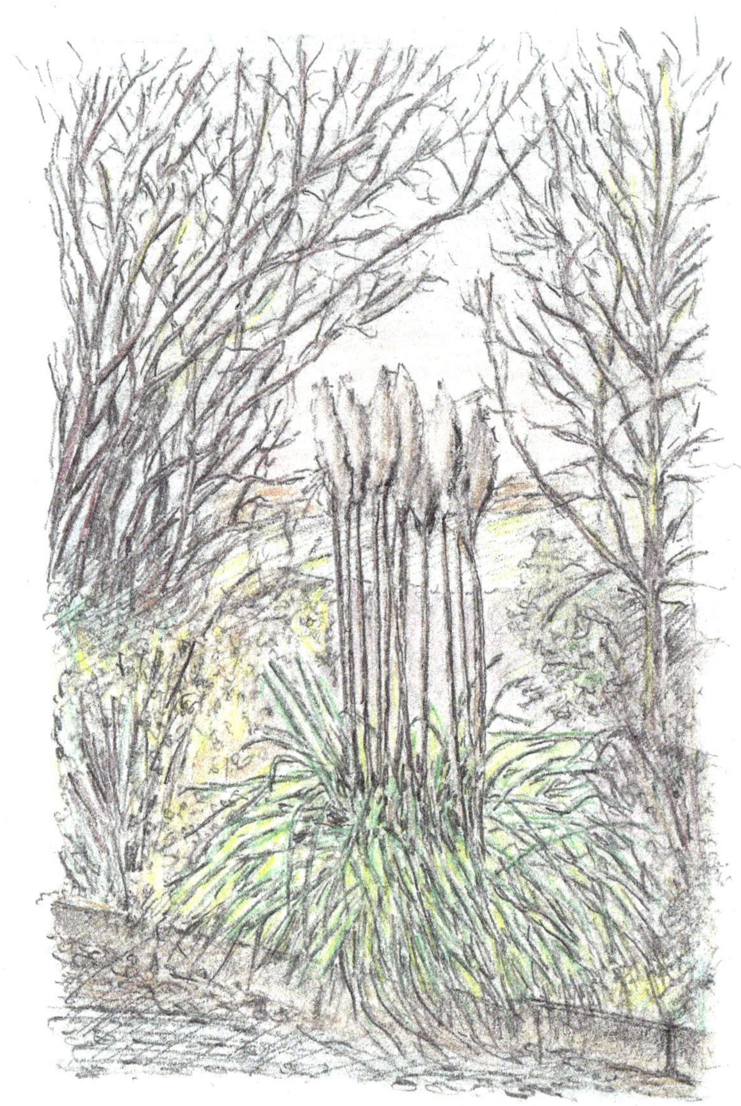

In the grounds of Henry Dixon Hall, Rivenhall, Essex, upon a border beside a field, sat these exuberant, impressive, pampas grasses, with their feathery flower head plumes, ornamental, with dense white panicles, gathered together like a group of visitors from another land, momentarily seeming out of place, strangers. Spidery pencil lines throughout to retain the powerful impact and presence of the bluish-green leaves.

15

Two solitary pines

Indifferent to us

Sway as one in the Spring breeze

Holding hands we watch.

Pillbox by the Chelmer

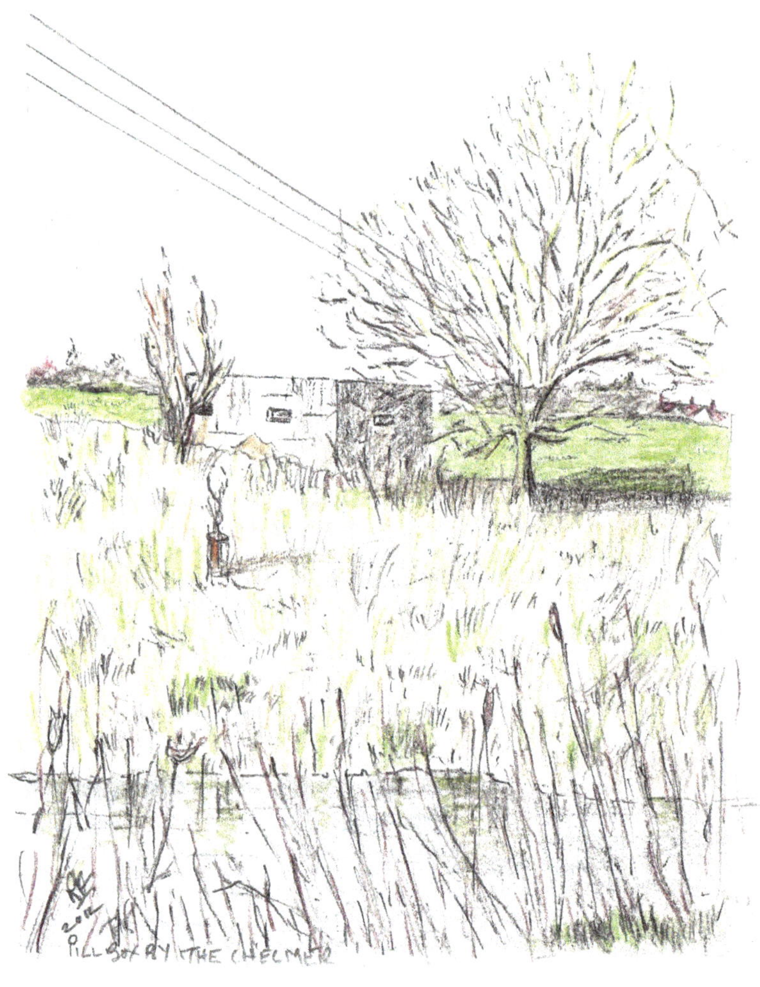

If you live near the Essex/East Anglian coast you will be very familiar with the small fortified field defences built in WW2 and known, because of their shape, as pillboxes, examples of the Home Front still remaining. The protective sleeve around the sapling is also providing a defence against invasion!

Brambles, by the Horse and Groom, Roxwell

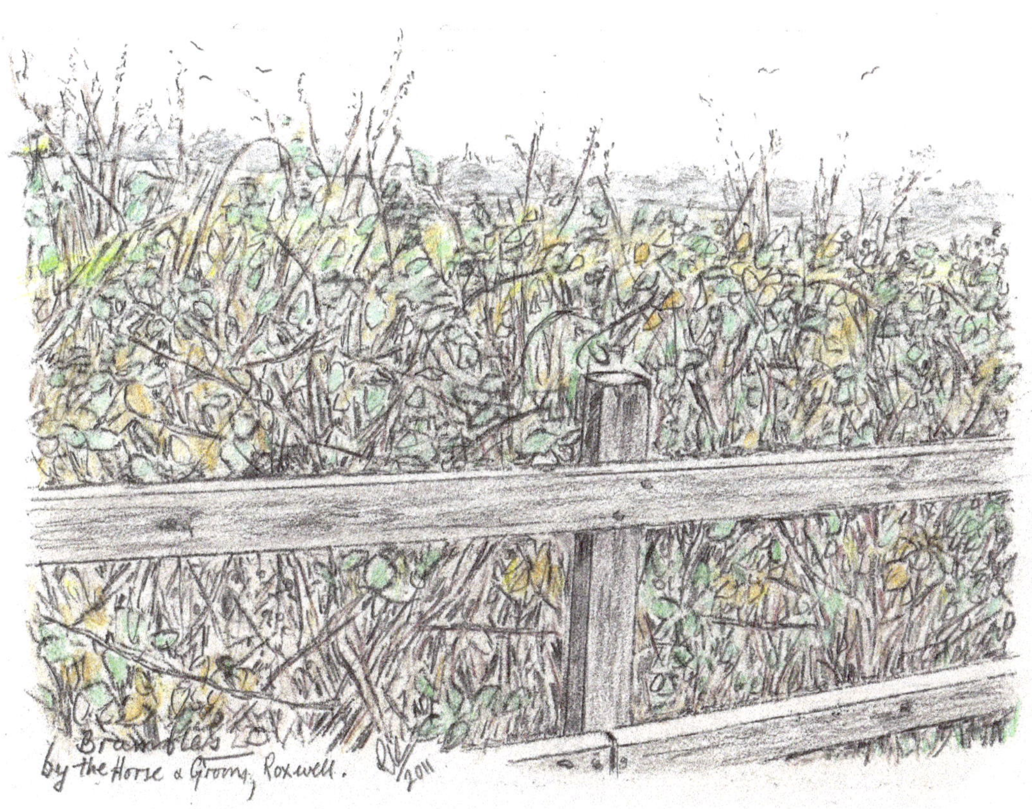

This hedge of brambles spoke 'go no further'. Trying to capture its density yet retaining definition was a real challenge, but very enjoyable, followed by a pub lunch.

16

We are guests today

Feel the Song of God

A world without shadow

Man and women One.

Welcome

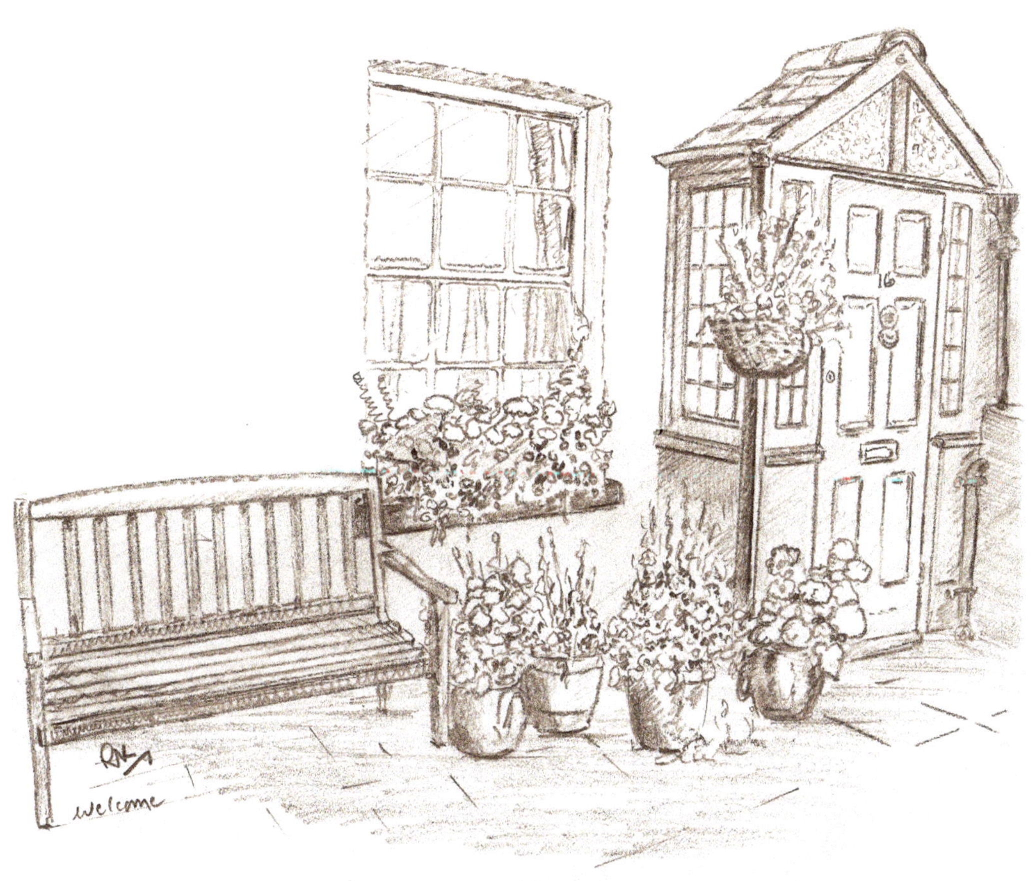

Here, the 'outside' is a reflection of the 'inside', welcoming and giving. Come, sit in peace, and watch the world go by.

17

Yes I acquiesce

To loves pain knowing

I will oft kiss your forehead

And receive true joy.

18

The candle's soft tears

Are this night for joy

A day-time of happiness

Your love like a flame.

Rosehips in the Hedgerow

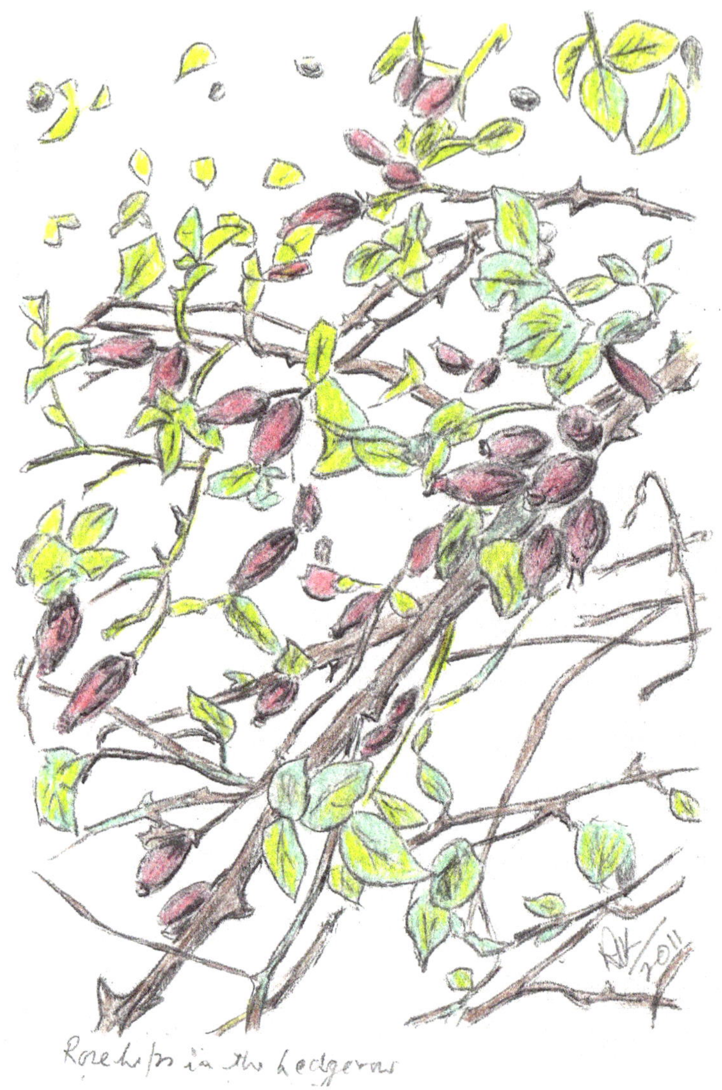

Tried to retrieve from the apparent 'muddle' of the hedgerow the rosehip's presence. As with many things in life, and certainly with drawing, it is often a question of having to decide 'what you leave in and what you leave out'. By bringing an openness to the process the imagination becomes liberated!

19

Enchanting Blackbird

Welcomes the Springtime

Your warm self-conscious laughter

Inspires tenderness.

20

How your existence

Penetrates my body

Like sunlight upon a prism

Spreading through my veins.

Danbury Woodland

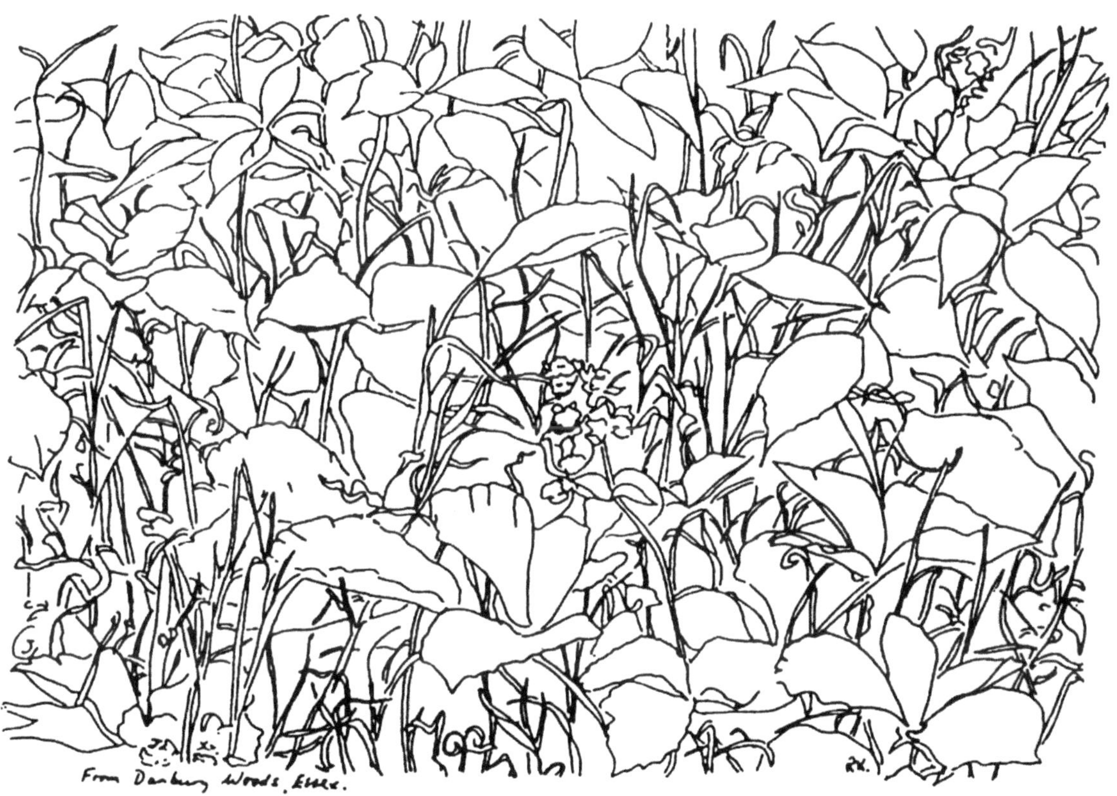

A line drawing in black ink, therefore no rubbing out of mistaken lines, serious concentration required, of this woodland scene. Patterns in nature everywhere.

21

Priceless, priceless gift

Of love's silken sap

Received by my blood-stream

You and I as one.

22

The four seasons turn

Without single pause

So it is that love expands

Unseen resolute.

Beside the River Can

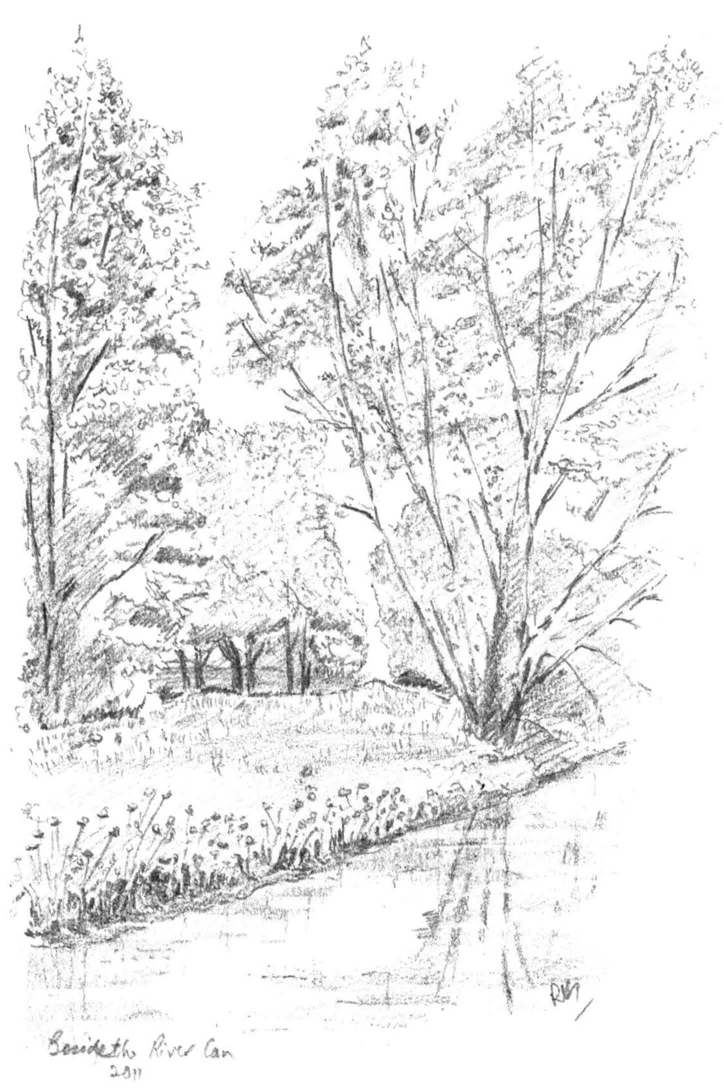

Sketched facing upstream as the River Can runs down to meet the River Chelmer in Chelmsford, County Town of Essex, to then join the River Blackwater and the North Sea. Tried to catch, on this Summer afternoon, the 'lightness' of air and scene, as the sun was moving rapidly to the west.

23

Like two silver threads

The rivers entwine

Reflecting both sun and moon

This mystical place.

A Working Sculpture

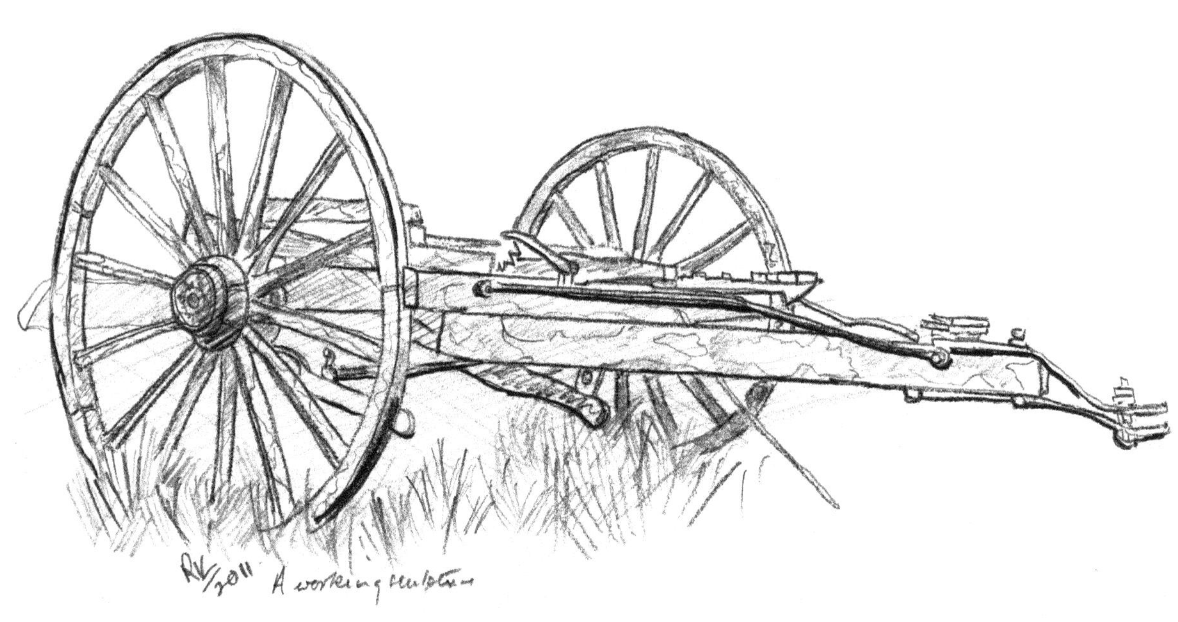

Could not believe my luck when I discovered this beautiful object 'begging' to be drawn. It is grand, like a fine sculpture, only more profound, as it worked for its meaning, its explanation. Real treasure, hidden behind a barn, incomplete, but whole, so very present.

Built beside the Med

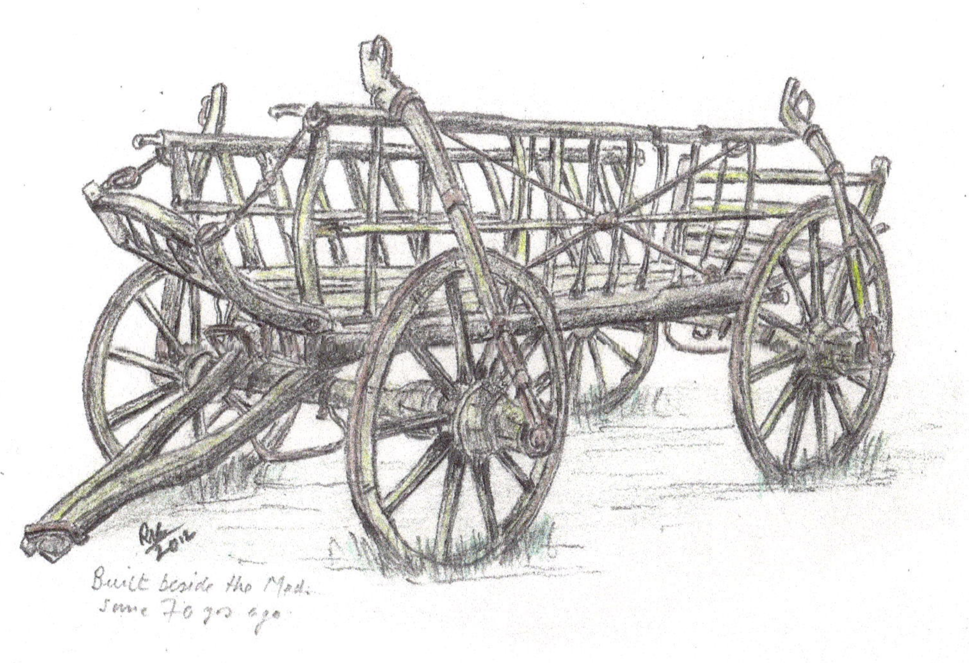

Discovered, with joy, this cart in a small field at Battlesbridge Antique and Craft Centre, Essex. Enquiries suggested it was built somewhere near the Mediterranean. The front wheels have a diameter of 2'6", rear 3'. Height 4'6", overall length 10', width 3'. The arms by the wheels drop downwards for extra load. Used soft colour to bring additional life and age to the drawing. (A few months later, in a nineteenth-century painting, at a gallery in Kracow, Poland, I saw a cart just like this one – I was amazed, and very pleased.)

24

Oh such joy pure joy

We kissed this day

I scream out I love you yes

And dance by the May.

Perfection in the Landscape

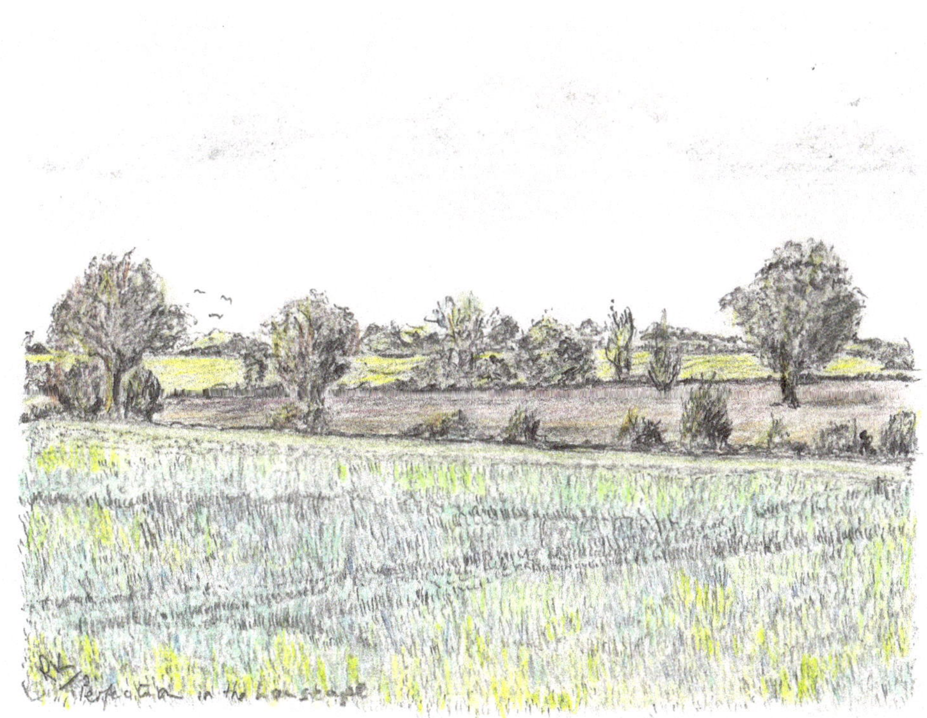

The luxuriant and fertile fields, the sounds of life and nature, bring an overwhelming presence. Trying to capture this with the use of pencils is indeed a challenge, and to feel part of this landscape is just perfect, in this world of wonder, and uncertainty.

25

Yesterday we hope

Now today we are

Late or soon I have to go

Time holds no reprieve.

26

Moving this page-mark

Of Forget-me-nots

Checks also months now passed

Since this gift you made.

Geranium Glory

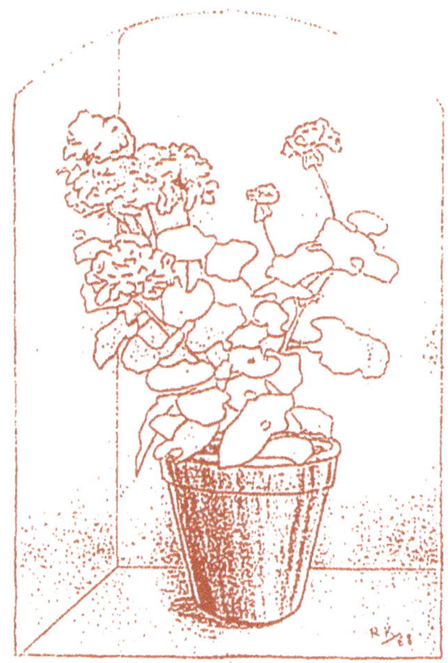

Geraniums, my friends in the garden, giving, unconditionally, in their vibrant colours. This drawing was originally drafted for a poster design, but was lost, only this small print remains, nevertheless I think the shapes are still 'alive and energetic', just like a memory.

27

Feel your breath you said

Reveal life's essence

Pulsing with the eternal

Deeper than our birth.

28

Breathing with Pure Land

Perfect in oneness

Gold carp in the August sun

Pierce the pool's surface.

Pure Land Meditation Centre

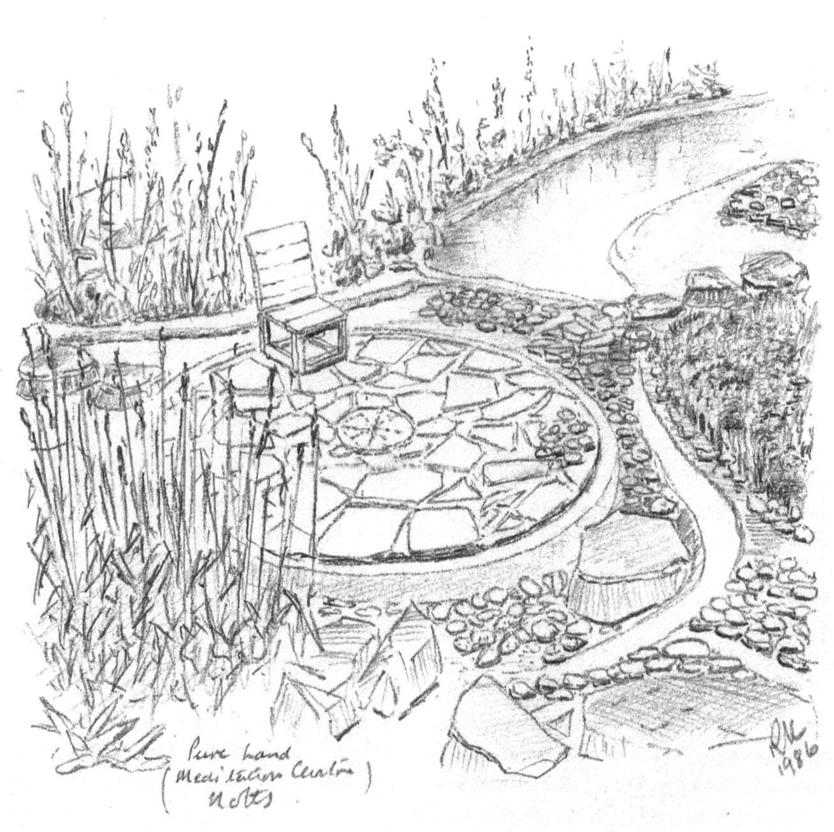

A place to discover the 'self' and 'oneness'. Tumbling, falling lines, letting go.

29

I love you today

More than yesterday

This most precious of all gifts

Such mystic meaning.

30

Pure white butterfly

On blue lavender

Blissful Japanese garden

An eternal song.

A Walk across an Essex Field

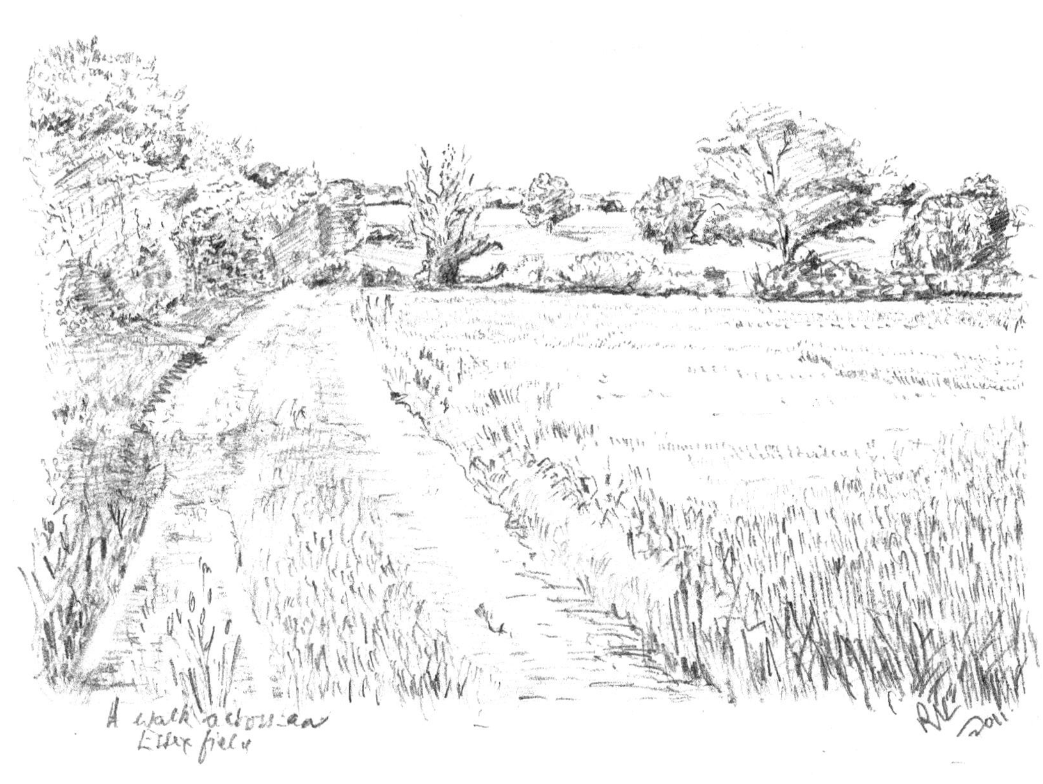

This is a favourite walk, across the fields, in this most English of landscapes. Reminds me of the importance, with given subjects, to be mindful of how the influence of light is retained and expressed, within the drawing. Allowing compassion, and that intuitive relationship with the subject, to direct us.

31

Golden wheat field edge

Together we lay

Never the world more perfect

Glowing like topaz.

Finished

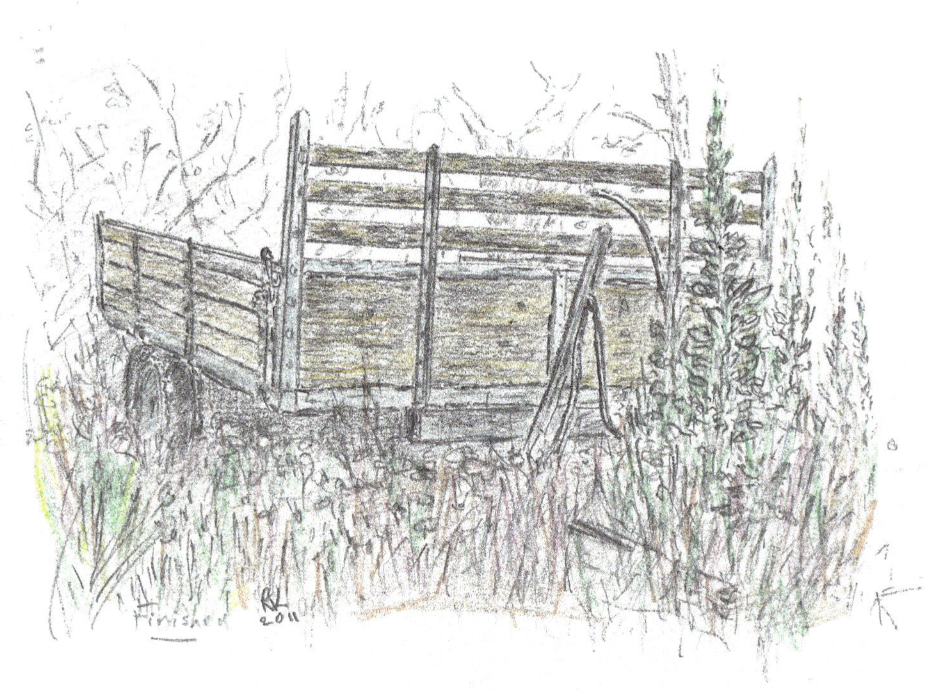

Symbolic of a time now passed, this abandoned trailer 'reached' out from the bushes. From the evidence of its faded colour it was easy to imagine it when new. With dedication and care it would be of use again, but sadly, I believe, it will remain forgotten in its place beneath the hedgerow.

Wrecked

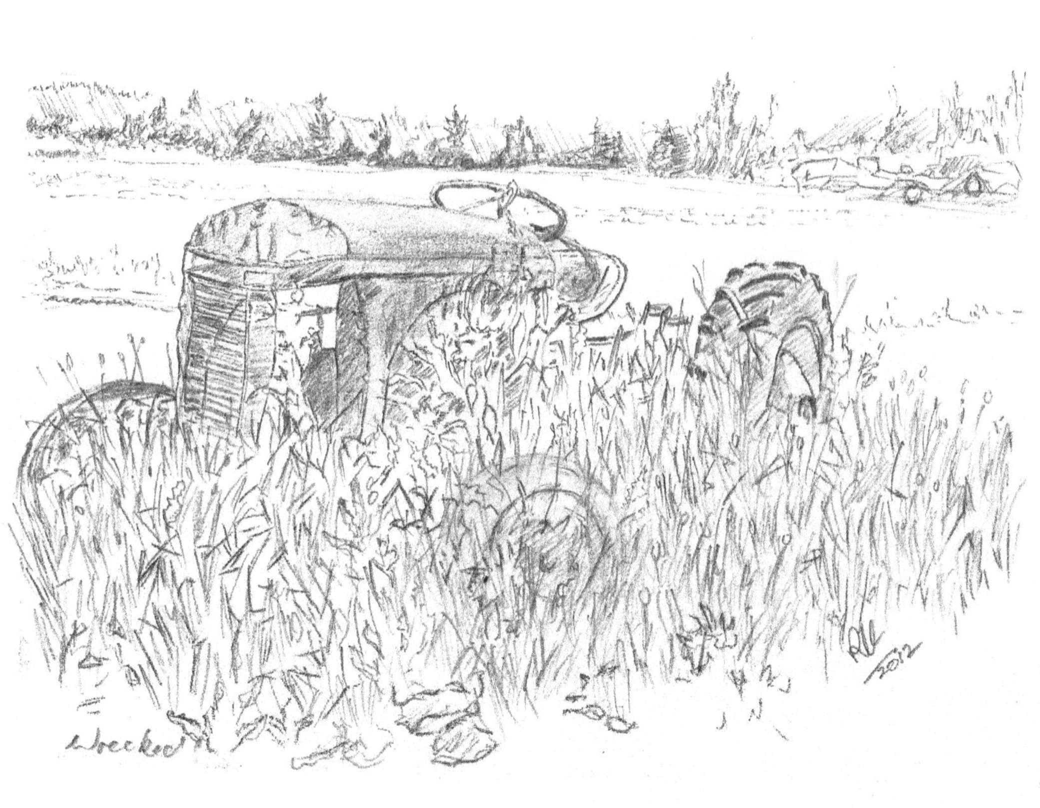

I first drew this Massey Ferguson tractor with a view from the opposite side, and returned a week later to draw again, but looking out across the fields. An image of determination and survival, left to simply be, in the fields where it must have worked. A most engaging image, giving expression to its own uniqueness.

32

Fragrant lemon balm

Voluptuous delight

Like the gentle Summer breeze

Secret breath of love.

Fruit Trees, Southern Spain

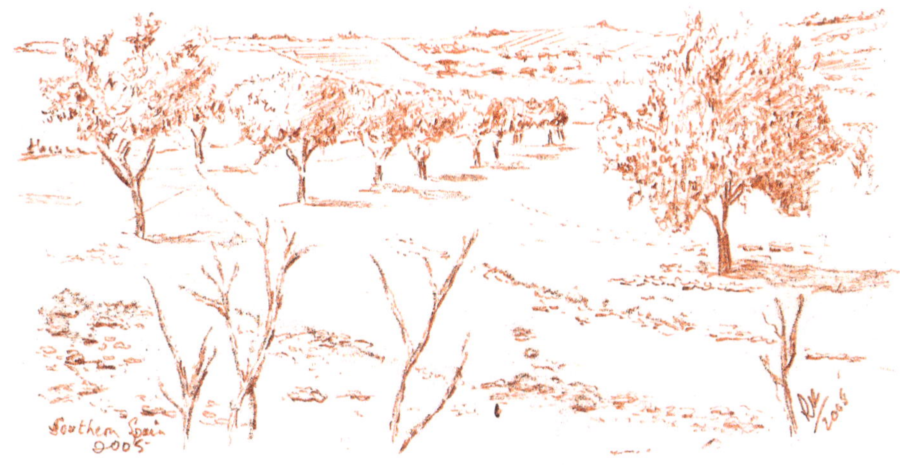

An open, and hot landscape, crackling in the Summer heat. I tried to engage by turning it red, in this land of the 'flamenco'.

33

Simple wooded chair

Welcoming, giving

Symbol and revelation

God within all things.

34

Leaden smell of earth

Pulsing garden heat

Rain falls on thick foliage

Fresh water colour.

Heybridge Basin

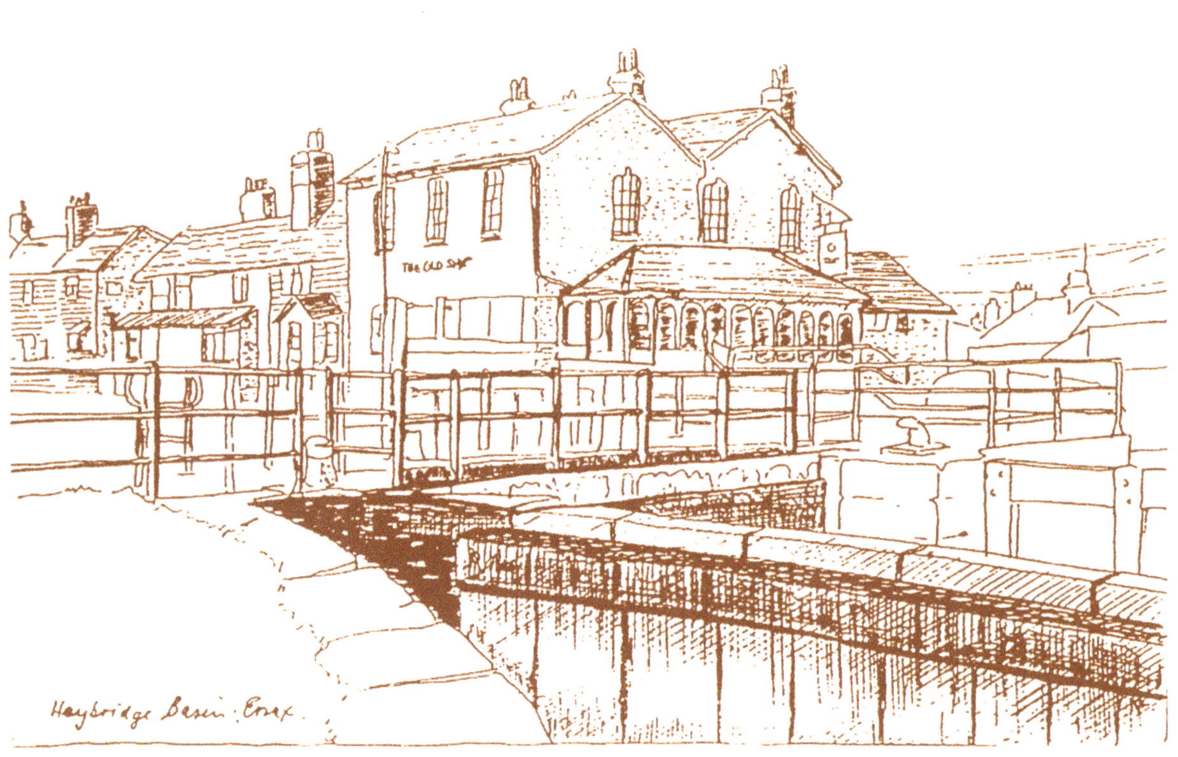

Drawing this complex of locks, and buildings beyond, was an exercise in perspective, also provided a perspective on life itself given the age of this place, its older industry of working barges long gone. Leisure craft are now moored upstream within the main lock waiting for the tide. The Old Ship public house displays lots of photographs from the old days.

35

Upon the sea wall

Beside the old lock

We crossed the proud threshold

Of our own selves.

36

Spinning glowing white

Inside my belly

Indestructible power

The source of all life.

Bog Wood, Six Thousand Years Old

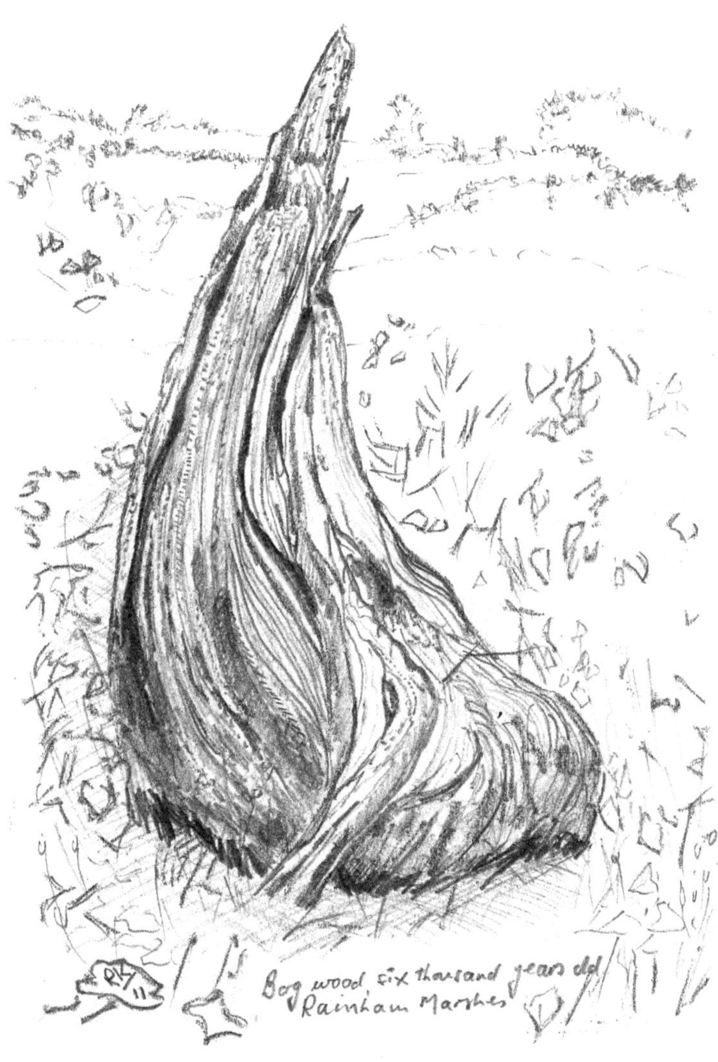

At the eastern edge of London the RSPB, thankfully, maintain this bird sanctuary in what is left of the Rainham Marshes. On display, in an open field for visitors to see, this piece of bogwood. The sight of a six thousand years old piece of wood took my breath away, and to draw it was like touching it, and in this place where Neolithic man once built their own primitive shelters.

37

Tranquil starry night

A silent witness

Listening to my heart beat

Pulse of the cosmos.

38

Love's keepsakes hidden

Trace moments gone

Stirring my soul like the wind

On the desert sand.

Near Coggeshall, Essex

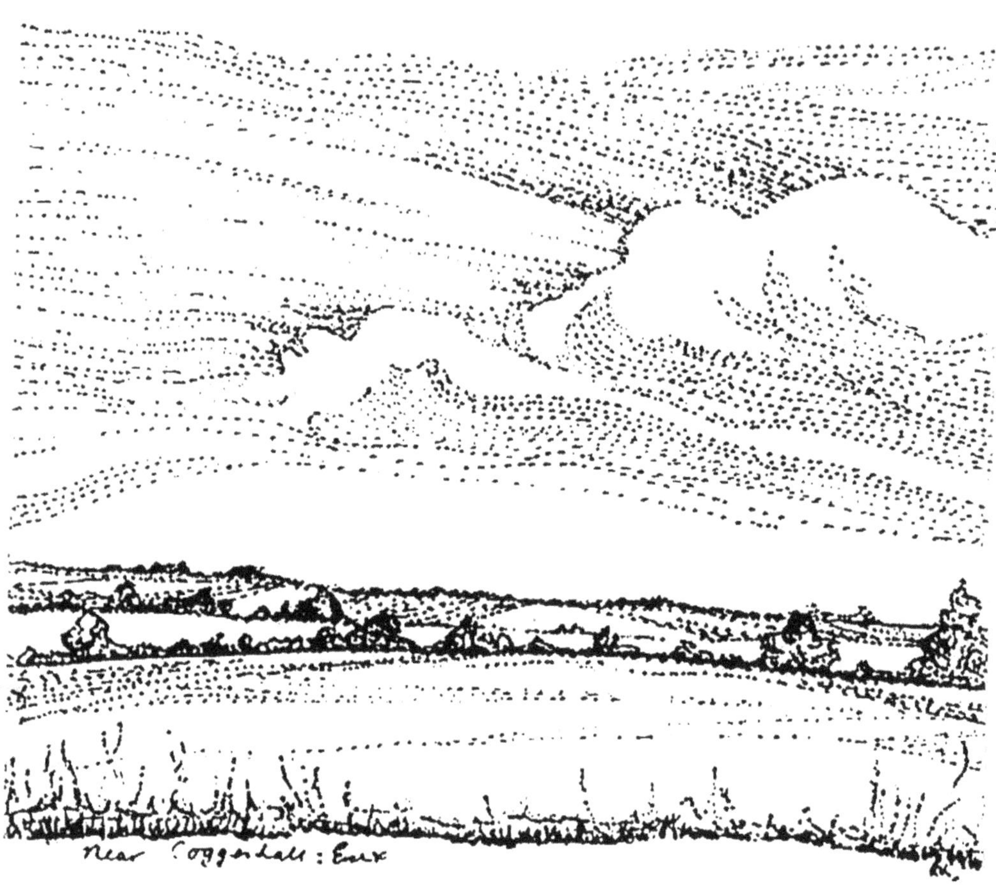

Here I tried to make a statement about the vast East Anglia skies, the source of light, unbounded space, by using dots to create a stylized image, emphasizing the movement of these clouds, and the dwarfed landscape.

39

Watching the sky change

Its halo of red

Moonlight on the window fell

Cool like porcelain.

Hollyhocks from My Garden

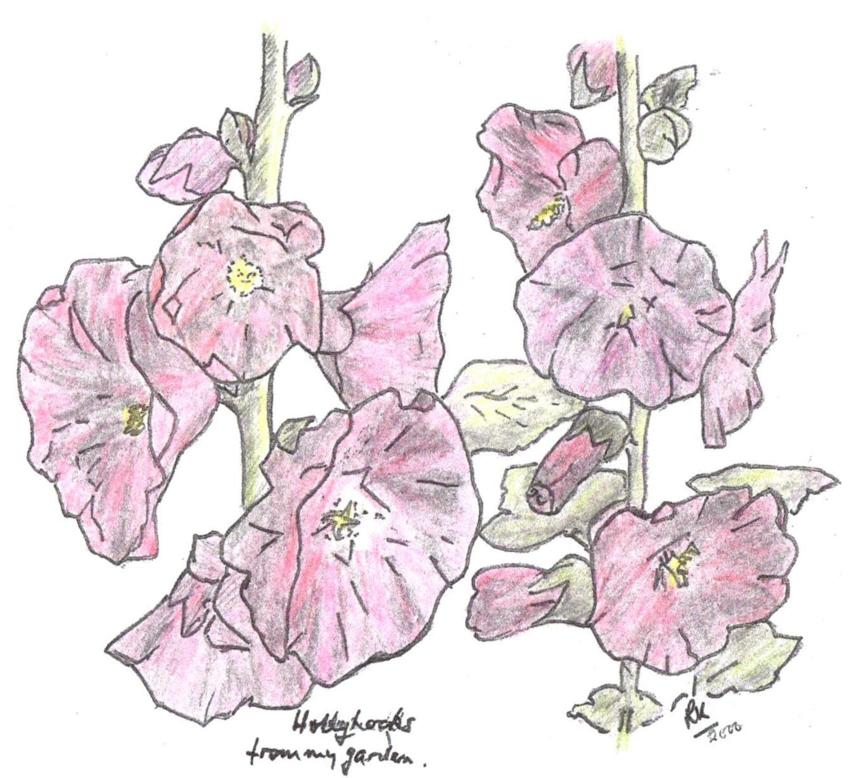

Flowers, as we know, are very good at 'speaking' for themselves, they are there with all their beauty, colour, fragrance. A joy to draw, and so many to choose from – what better way of meeting the natural world, with all its complexity, subtlety, and form!

Foxglove Glory

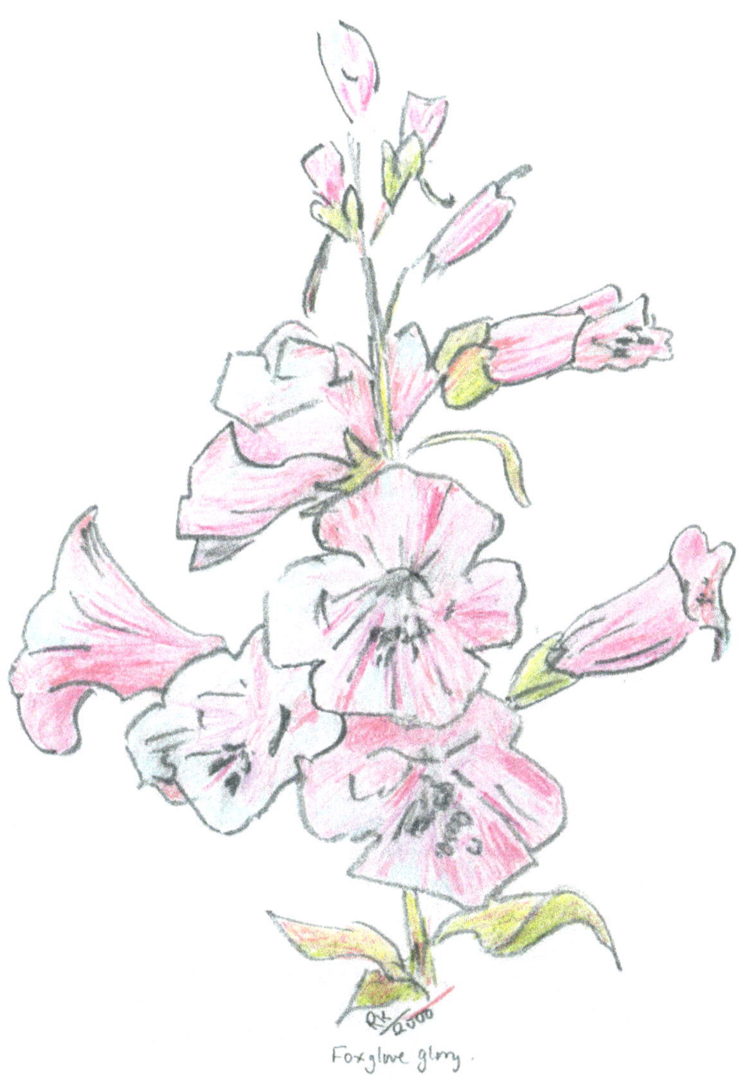

Drawn using a fine-point pen and coloured pencils – tried to achieve a crisp, illustrative appearance.

40

Land wrapped in snow

As the sunlight cools

Fire in the aged fireplace

Warmth and well-being.

Alone

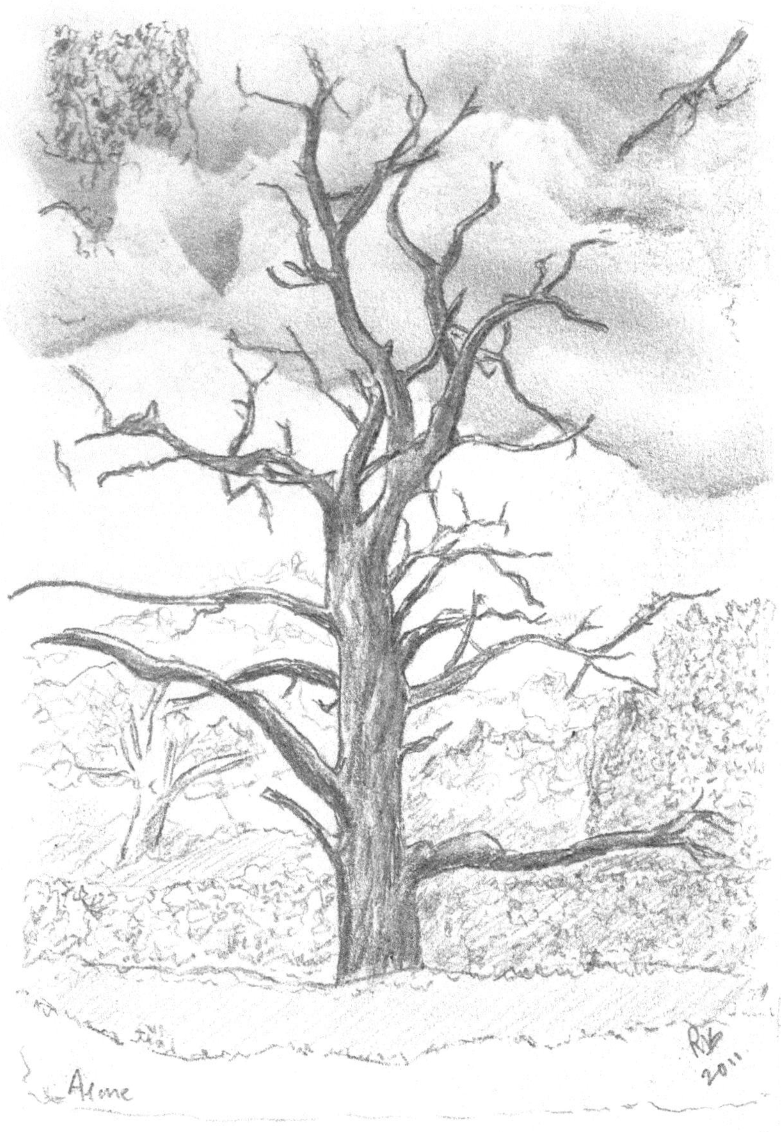

This dying tree, alone, the shapes had me thinking of cartoon images – dramatic, threatening, scenic, forceful – with an imposing and evocative sky. Drawn at Langdon Hills country park, near Basildon. Added blue pastel in order to give the sky more depth and movement.

41

At your sacred font

Soft petals murmur

Melody of creation

This song of heaven.

42

Pure life giving air

Where the Avon floods

Time for flowering and growth

Within this stillness.

Danbury Woods

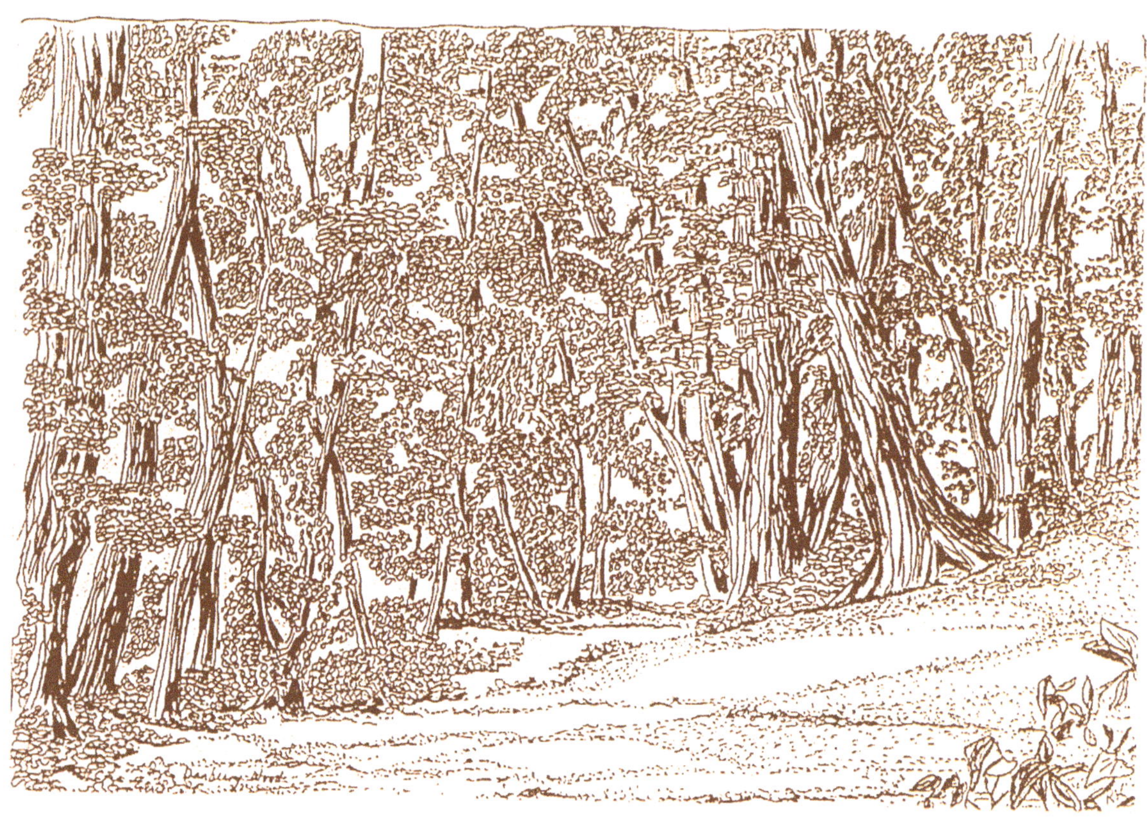

Spent many happy hours walking and playing in these woods, with children, and grand-children. (Also known locally as the bluebell woods, springtime scent and colour, an oasis of purple/blue, immediate, not to be missed.) Drawn using a simple technique, suggesting the fun and playfulness associated with these woods.

43

Flowers give their love

And slowly perish

As selfless as the salt wind

Blowing from the sea.

44

Sitting in stillness

Absorbing closeness

A transcendent ecstasy

Bliss of unity.

Line-drawing of Table and Chairs

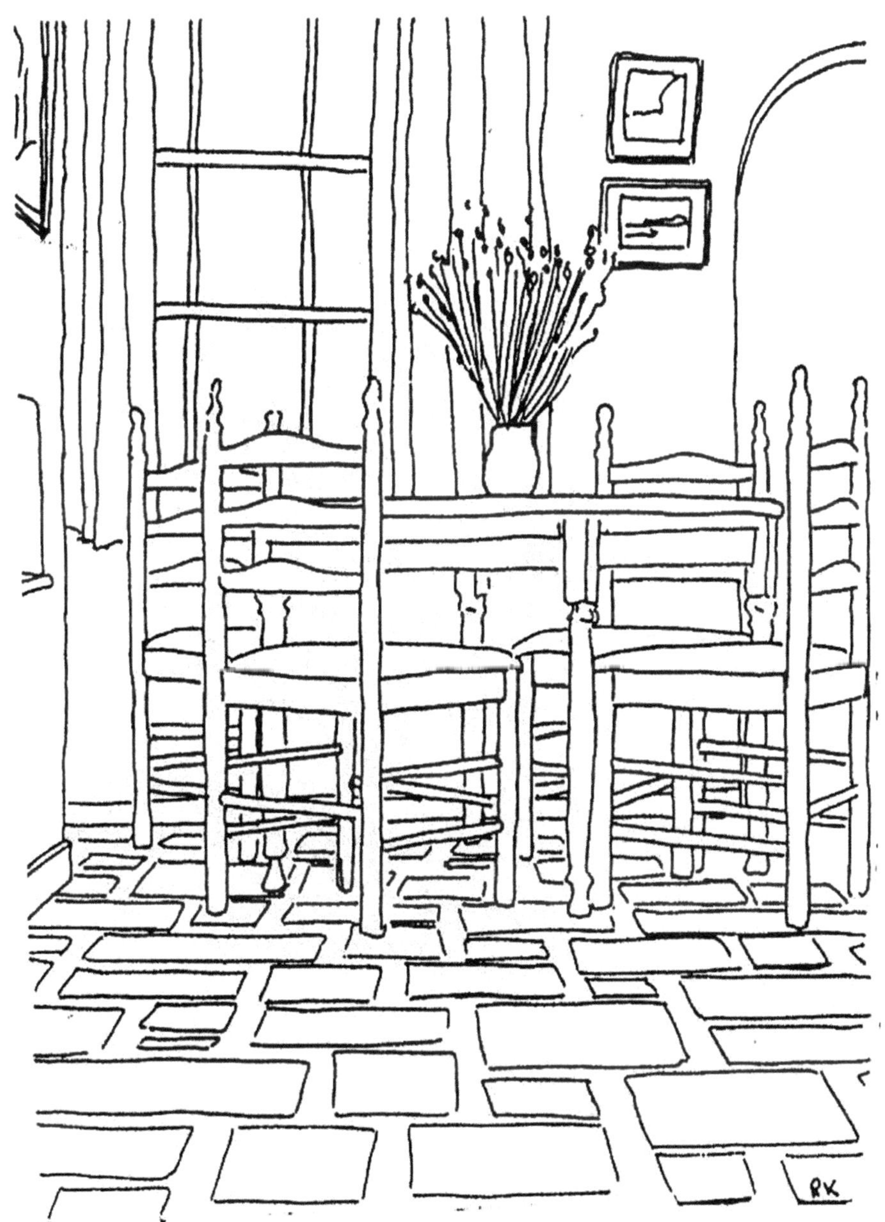

This subject invokes for me family life, the value of order, security, a simple scene given life and energy through the flowers in the vase – now waiting for the individuals to again take their place at the table… reassembling, to make complete their picture, in their own individual way.

45

Faint scent of snowdrops

In late Winter sun

Not a single word spoken

This thrill of living.

46

Helping to prepare

This evening meal

Living tempered by being

A truth won from life.

Grasses

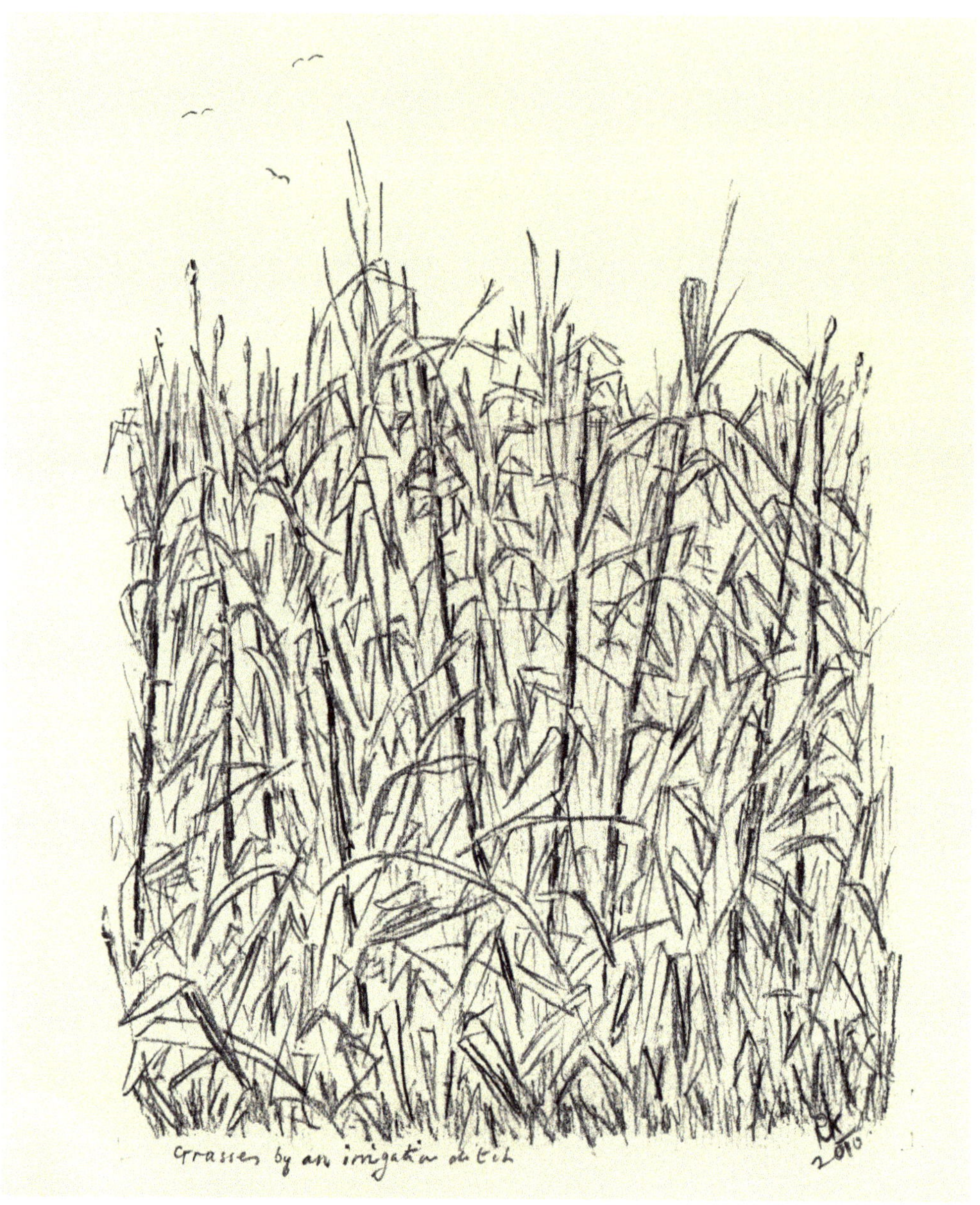

These beautiful reeds and grasses were growing beside an irrigation ditch in Spain – the shapes of the leaves reminded me of the effect achieved in Chinese paintings by using a pointed brush held vertical to the paper surface. I can still hear these grasses rustling in the warm wind. Used mainly a 3B pencil, on tinted paper.

47

Beneath the coarse grass

Sparkling Celandine

This blissful day among days

Unveiled before us.

When I was a Boy

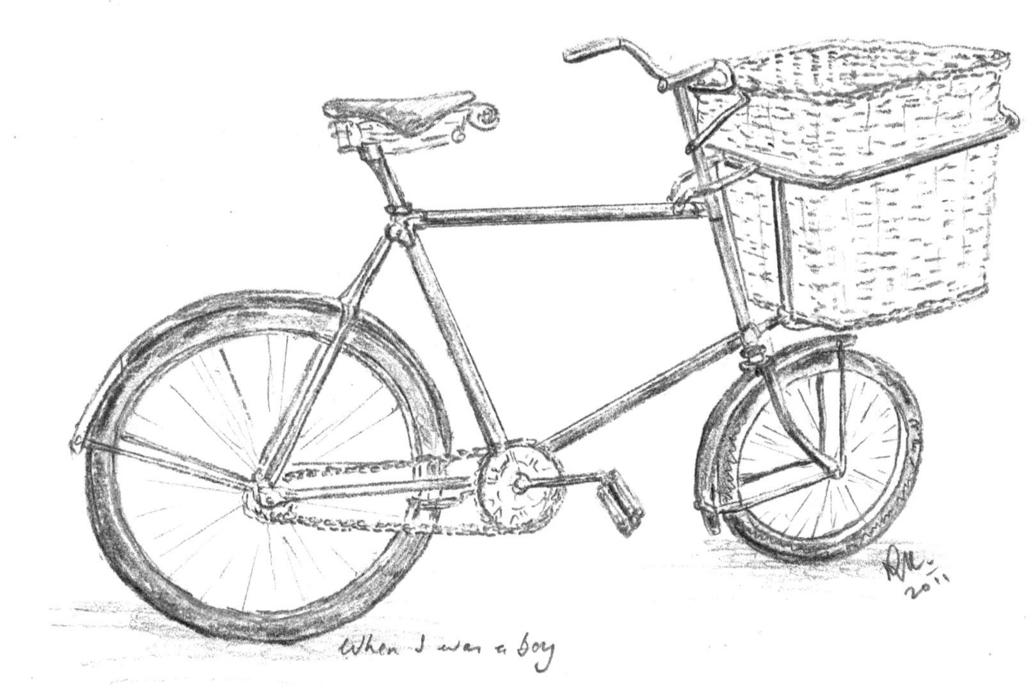

Saw this old delivery bike at an agricultural show in East Anglia – just like the one I rode, when I was a boy, for our local butcher every Saturday (for four years). Those formative experiences! My tribute to youth, innocence, simplicity. Especially enjoyed finding a way to suggest the basket, and not have to lift it!

A Mountain of Years

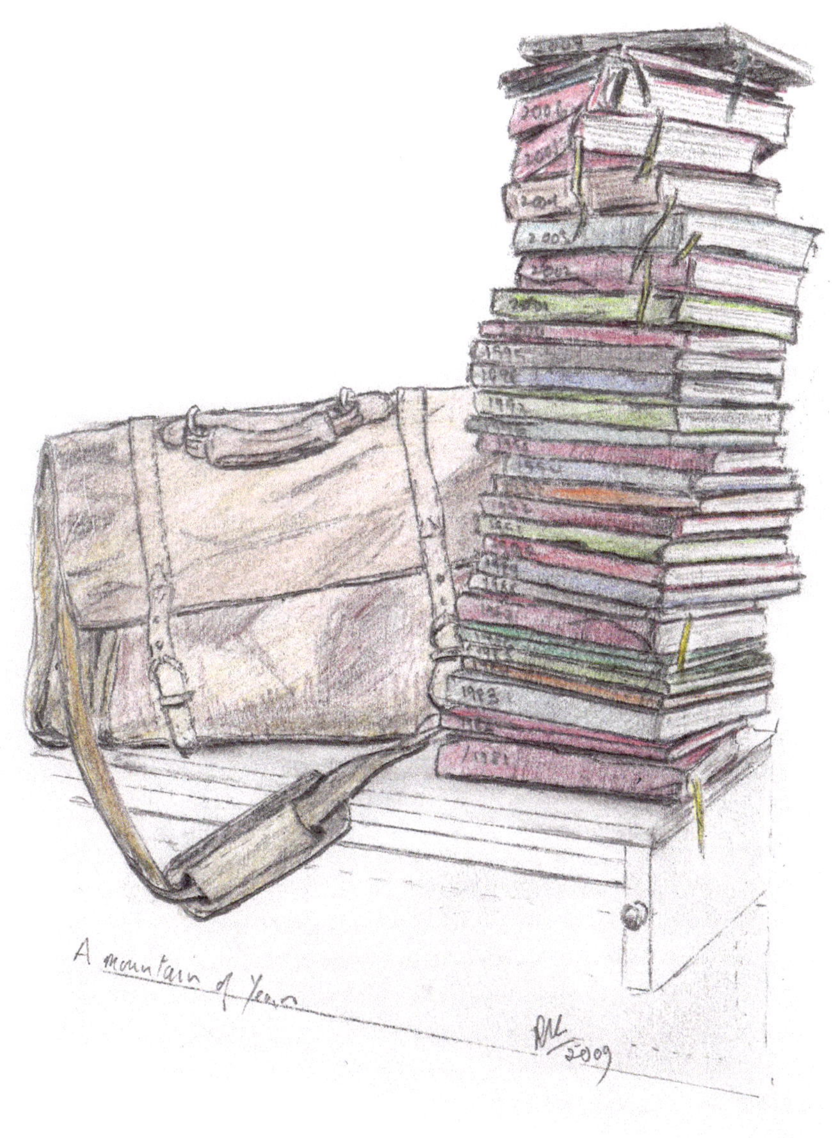

A pile of old work diaries. A different way of recording time. Contained an uncanny and pitiless feedback as I 'revisited' those spent years.

48

Coming of age

Under aged beams

Supported by divine truth

As fate moves unseen.

The Old Abbey Gardens, Bury St Edmunds

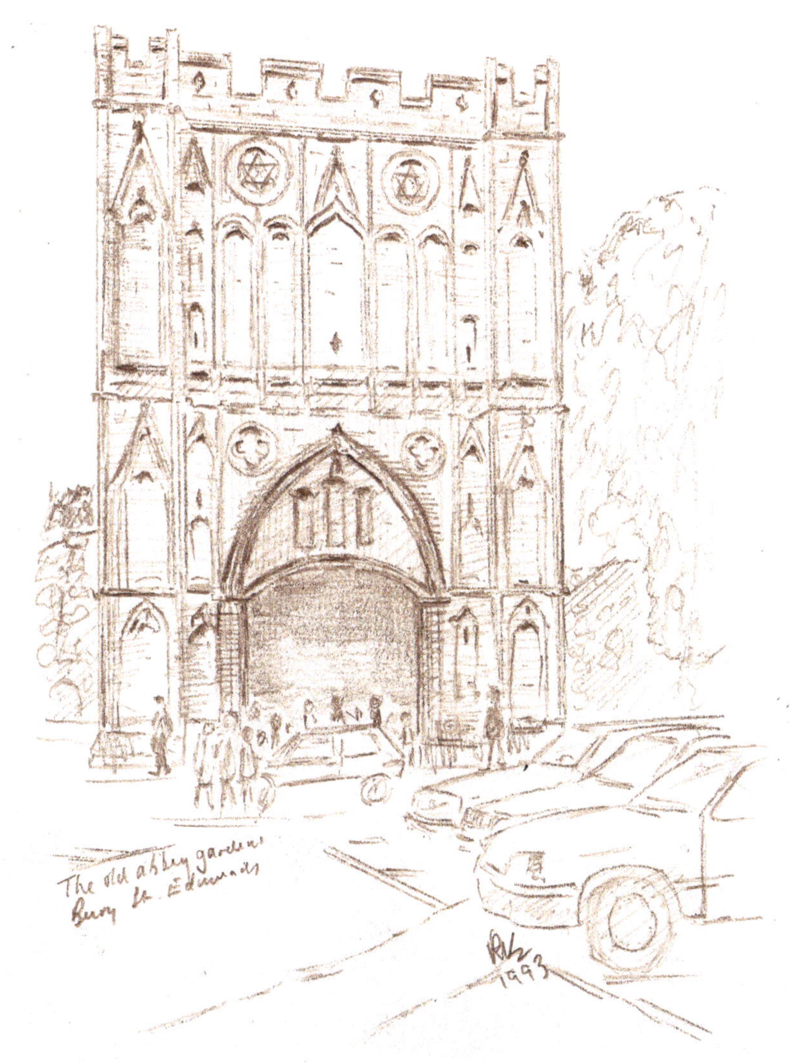

This magnificent entrance was built in the 1300s. In these gardens a plaque marks the place where in 1214 the then Cardinal and twelve Barons swore an oath that changed our history. Seven months later King John was compelled to sign The Great Charter of the Liberties of England, one of the greatest constitutional documents of all times giving us our right to contest unlawful imprisonment. Sketching in some visitors also gives an idea as to the scale of this entrance… and those events.

49

A dawn of delight

This fine Good Friday

Our spirits will rose to find

That path to safety.

50

Your smile recaptured

In sweet violets

Like an ageless bloom I hold near

So fine and precious.

A Retreat

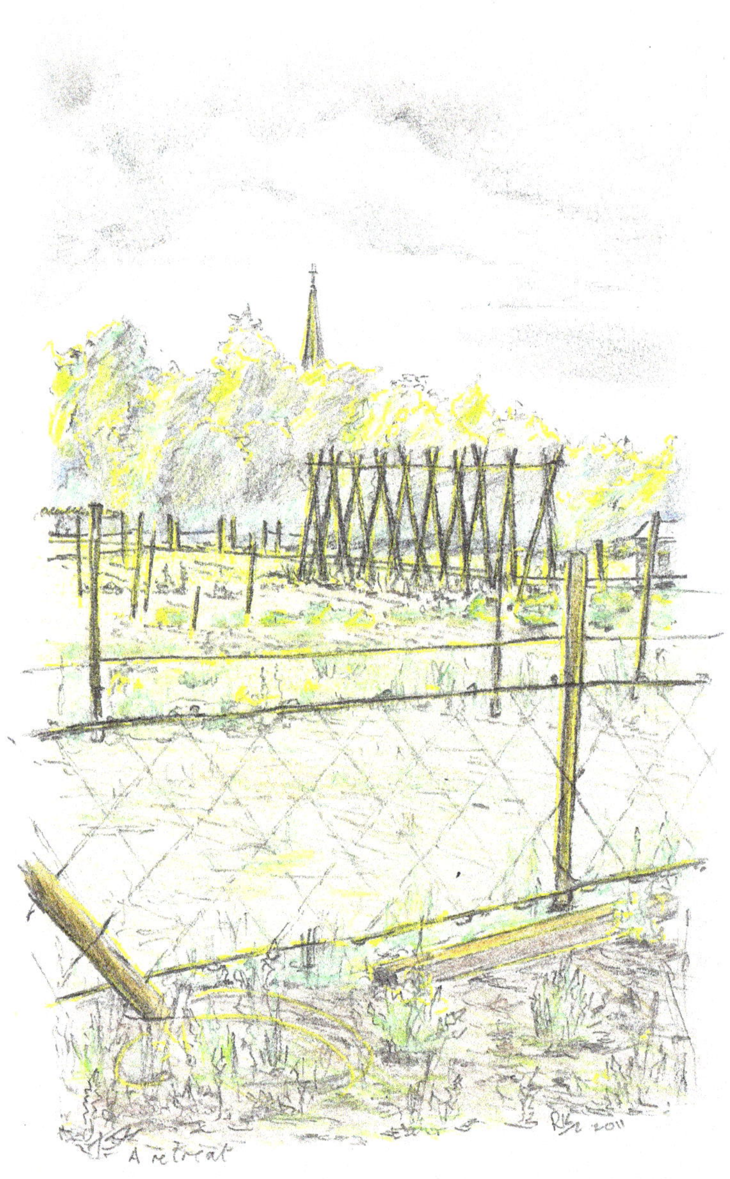

The church spire became a critical part of this composition, adding to the serenity. (Allotments, usually a place away, appear to provide a sense of retreat.) I was reminded of the quiet times, spent as a child, in our kitchen garden at home and tried to recall, recapture, that same benevolence and safety.

51

Heat-haze suspended

Above early crops

A moment among many

Giving us new life.

52

Ev'rything you do

Touches my sense

Like the fragrant bluebell wood

The cuckoo's sweet song.

Somerset Woods 2007

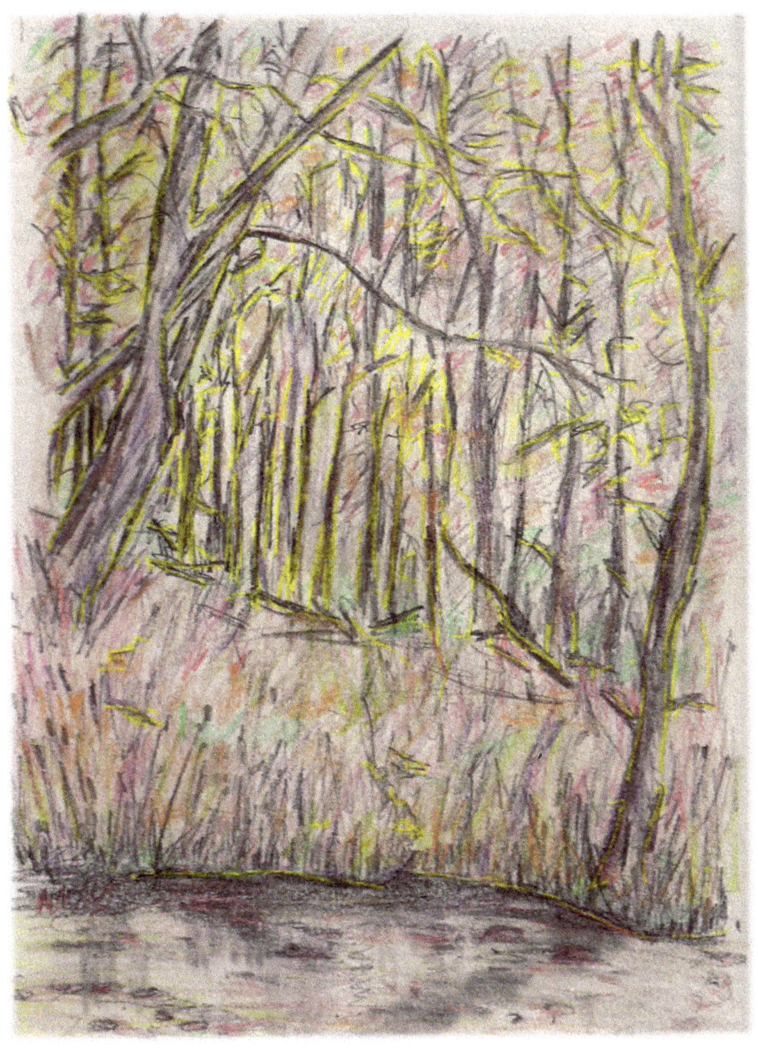

An Autumn day walk in the Quantock Hills, Somerset. Sketched quickly, using coloured pencils, trying to catch an impressionistic feel to this dense and colourful woodland scene.

53

Lush sparkling leaves

In May's dense garden

Illuminating an hour

Spent in solitude.

54

Through the night we live

To sunlight's beauty

The day knows when to dawn

That is life's nature.

The Chelmer Blackwater Canal, Little Baddow

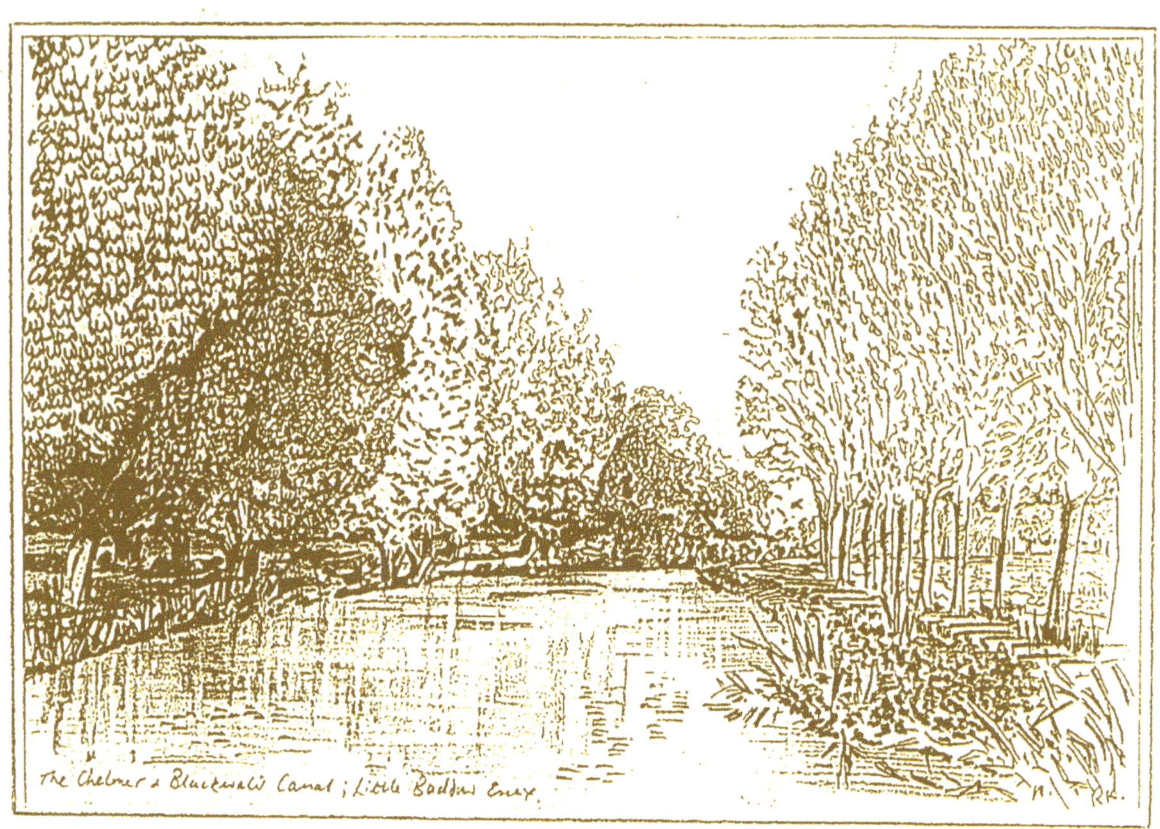

The majority of these varied, self-contained, and imposing trees, were blown down by the hurricane that hit the south and east of England in 1987 (an estimated 15 million others were blown down or felled as they had become unsafe). This drawing now feels like a tiny monument to the trees lost, that October!

55

Oh praise laburnum's

Shape and golden hue

A form containing all worlds

Ourselves in all things.

Built in the Early 1900s

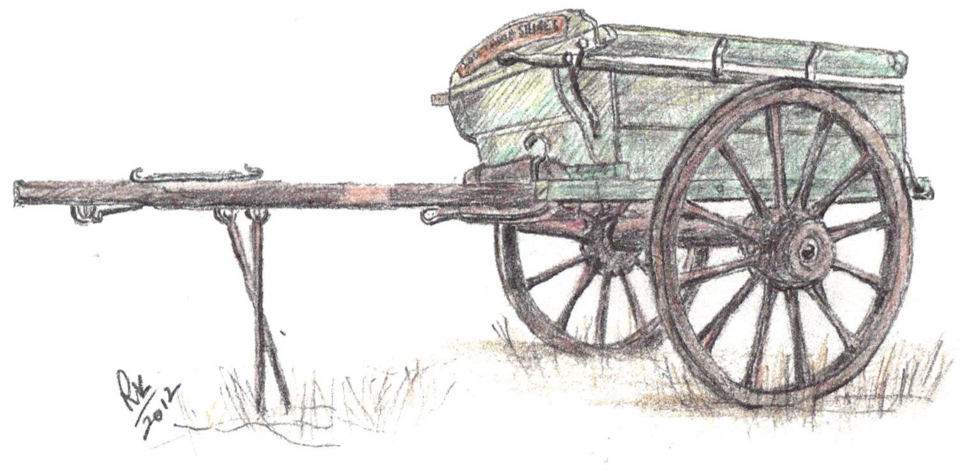

A romantic image, no doubt! Design, build, scale, versatility, carts like this one were used for centuries. In drawing this I tried to make it as solid and determined as it appears, and is. Colour, I believe, adds to its presence.

The Rake

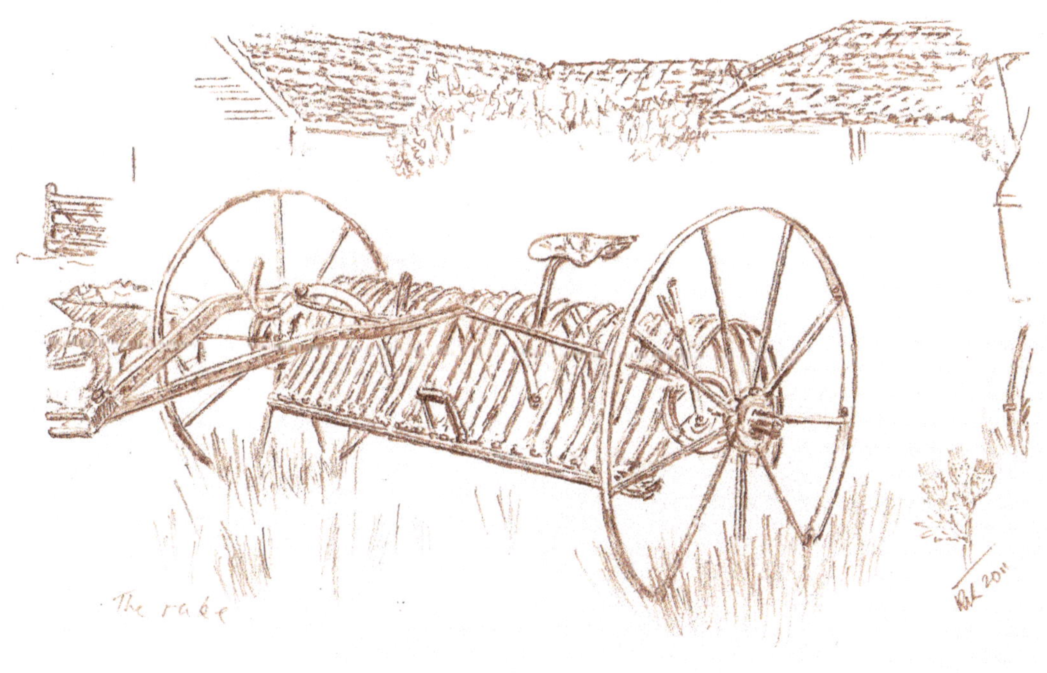

A perfect-looking machine. The difficulty in drawing it was in ensuring it looked made out of metal and not wood. The secret was in the refinement of the wheels. Particularly enjoyed suggesting the farm buildings, and bits and pieces about.

56

The wind-chime of cast stone

And far seaside shell

Brings freshness and gaiety

To the silent room.

Beehives Sketch

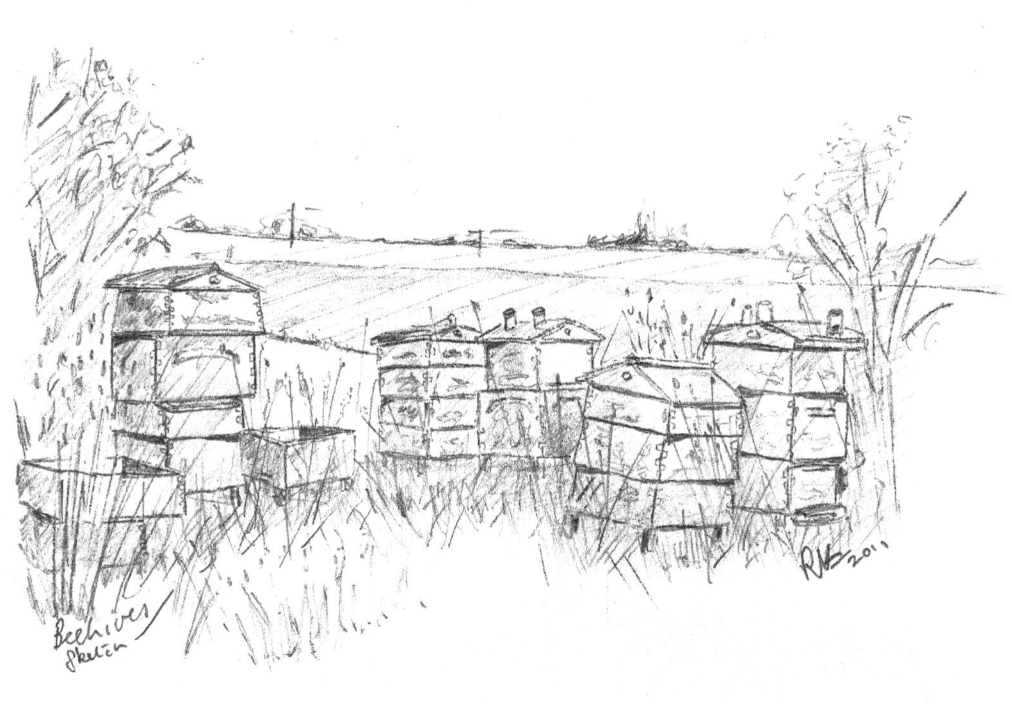

Walking along the headland of a field, stumbled across (not into!) these beehives. Great subject for drawing. Moreover, there was an association with my father who kept bees as a hobby, with his good friend Peter Mzyk (who escaped from Hungary during the 1956 uprising, and was subsequently befriended by my family). Beekeeping, as we know, has a real connection with the natural world, pollination, growth, production, harvest, the seasons, paying attention… just like drawing from nature!

57

Amid squandered years

Deepest comfort found

In this hour by the river

The first day of June.

58

Low wayside cottage

Housing faded dreams

A home for generations

Now still like marble.

Boreham Oak

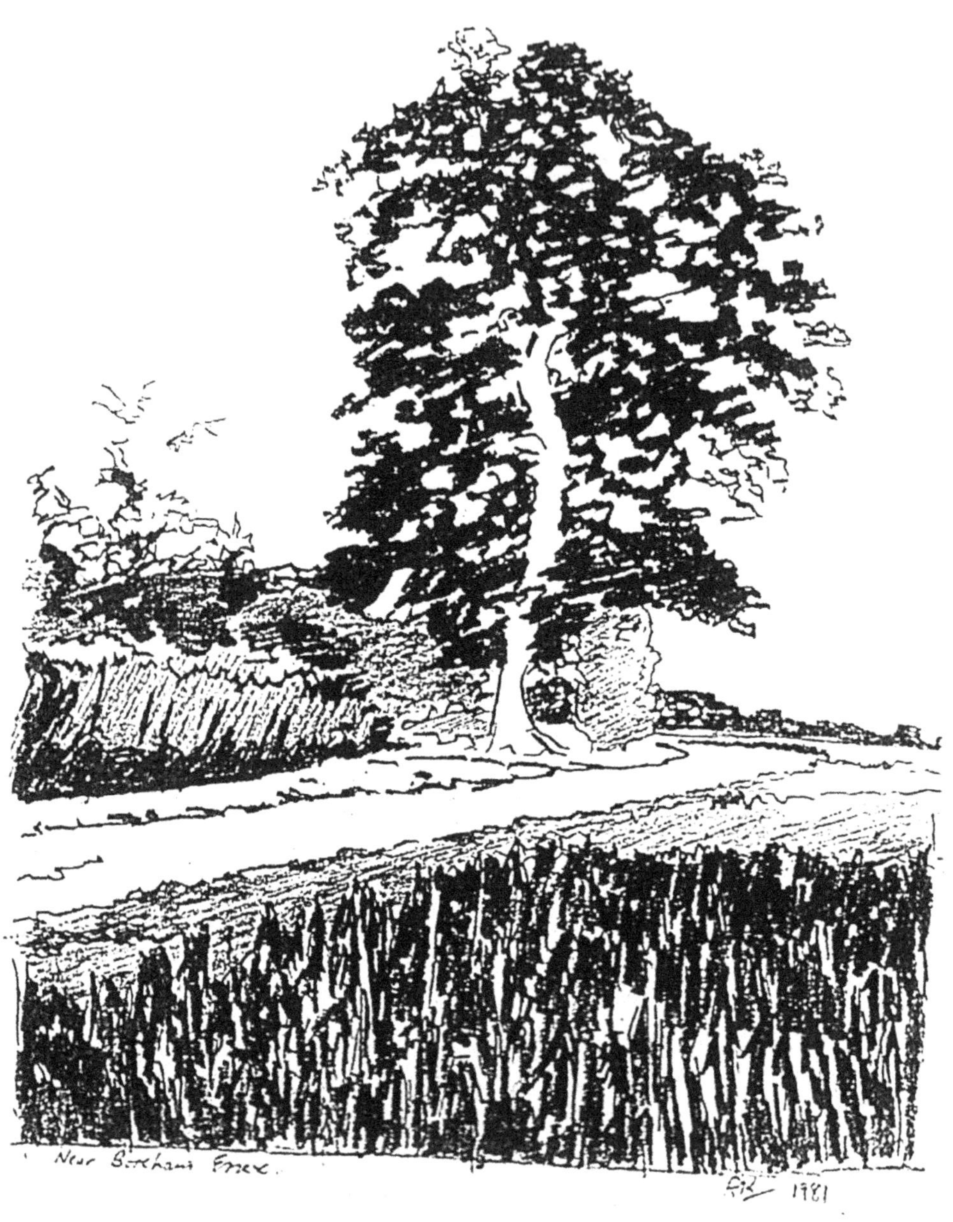

Discovered by chance this footpath into the countryside. Also discovered, in the full bloom of youth, this oak tree. Visited again, 25 years later, and was so very pleased to find the tree had survived storm, drought, and life. Older and wiser, certainly. Pure joy, to hug again, this special friend.

59

An island of light

From the window glows

Absorbed by the shapeless dust

Whence all life is born.

60

Whatever exists

Contains perfection

The silence before parting

The joy of meeting.

Autumn

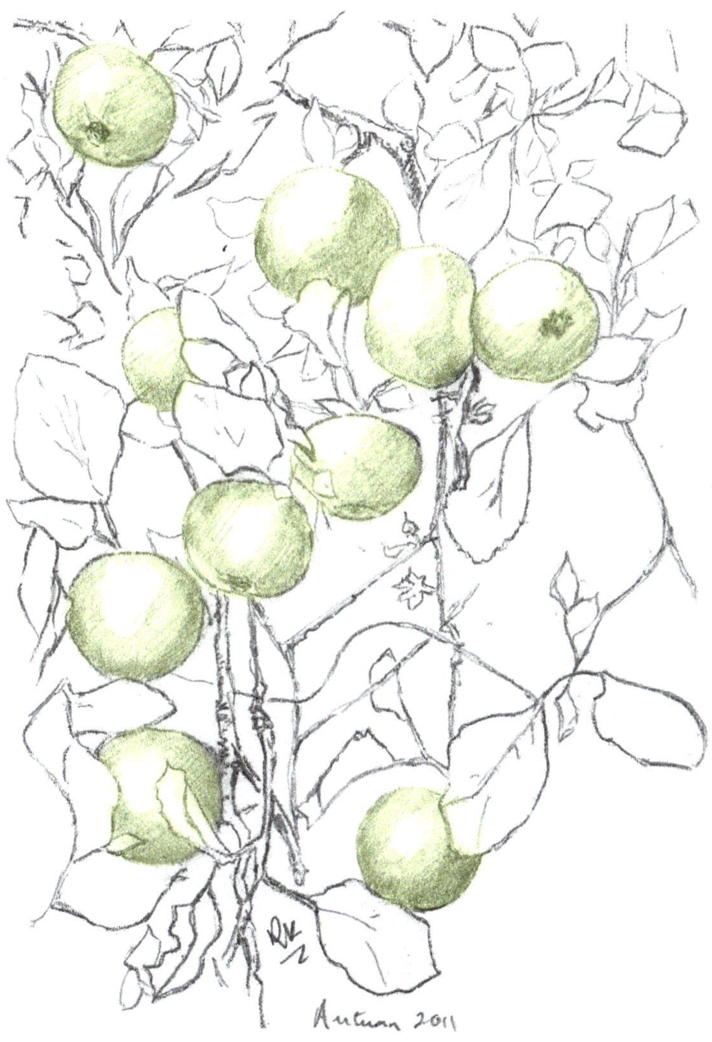

Sketched from the apple tree at the end of our daughter's garden. Lush shapes. Highlight upon the apples provides form and freshness. Imagination and observation provide the direction and meaning to any composition. The light green adds to the flavour!

61

A thousand pebbles

Sing with the river

Creation's glorious song

Of infinite grace.

62

Take this humble gift

Of limestone crystal

And hold a million souls

Life everlasting.

Ickwell Bury Woods Bridge

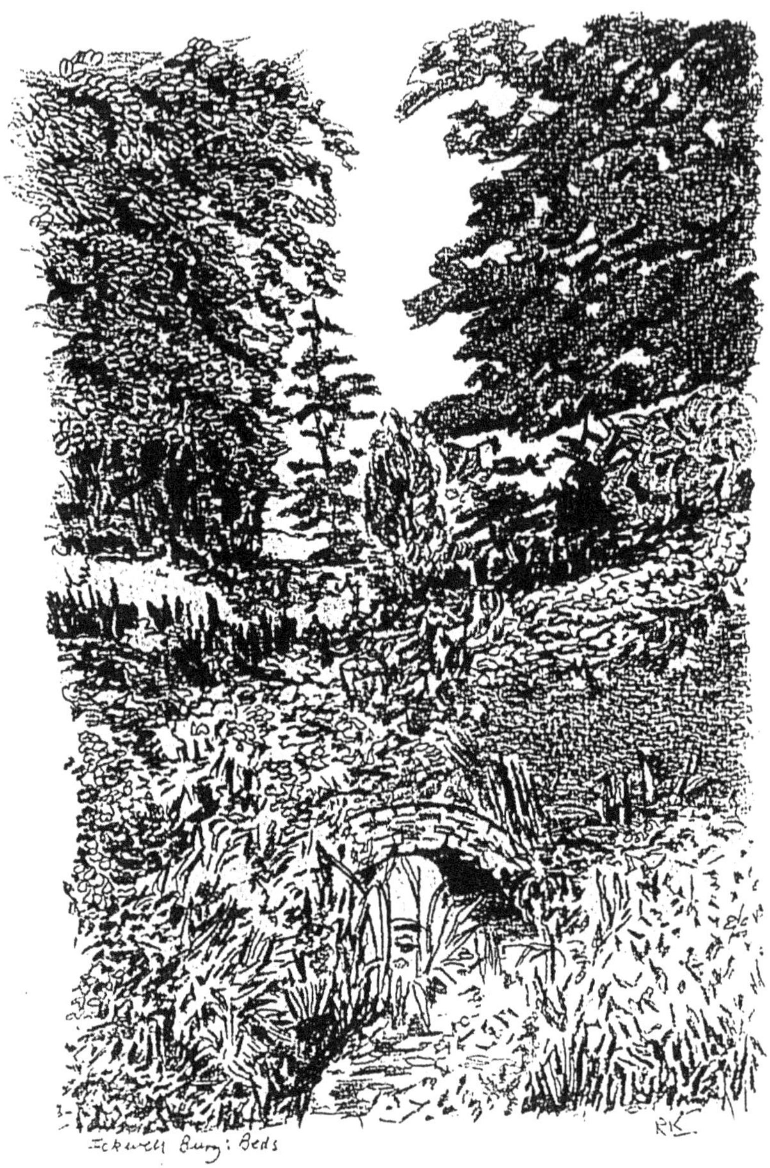

Originally drawn 'In the dark', now with the sun behind me, a variety of foliage, sensitive nuances of light, tried to capture the feel of an engraving, to give the impression of age, in this ancient woodland. (The Yoga for Health Foundation used to be in Ickwell.) The deeper I looked at these leaves, it felt like I was drawing an image from creation itself, in a different space, and no longer an image from nature alone.

63

Between your branches

Infant cherry tree

The eternal law proclaims

Patient communion.

Hedge Dark and Light

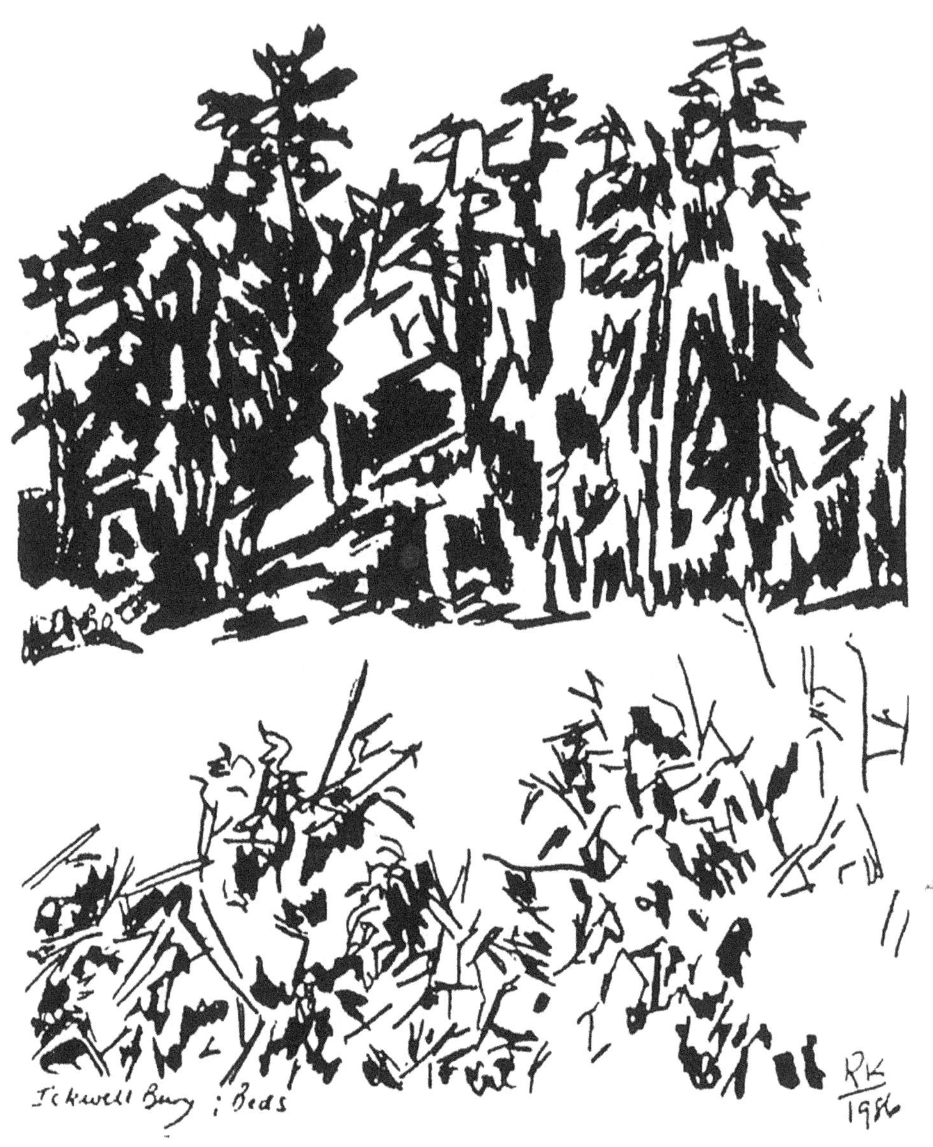

Beside the lake. A place of beauty, harmony, peace. Tried to achieve the vitality of ancient Chinese landscape paintings, with an economy of line (like calligraphy). The very absence of detail can itself create rhythm by giving prominence to the main subject – being alike yet unlike that subject – and by finding a 'sturdy simplicity' within the composition.

Ickwell Bury Nature Reserve

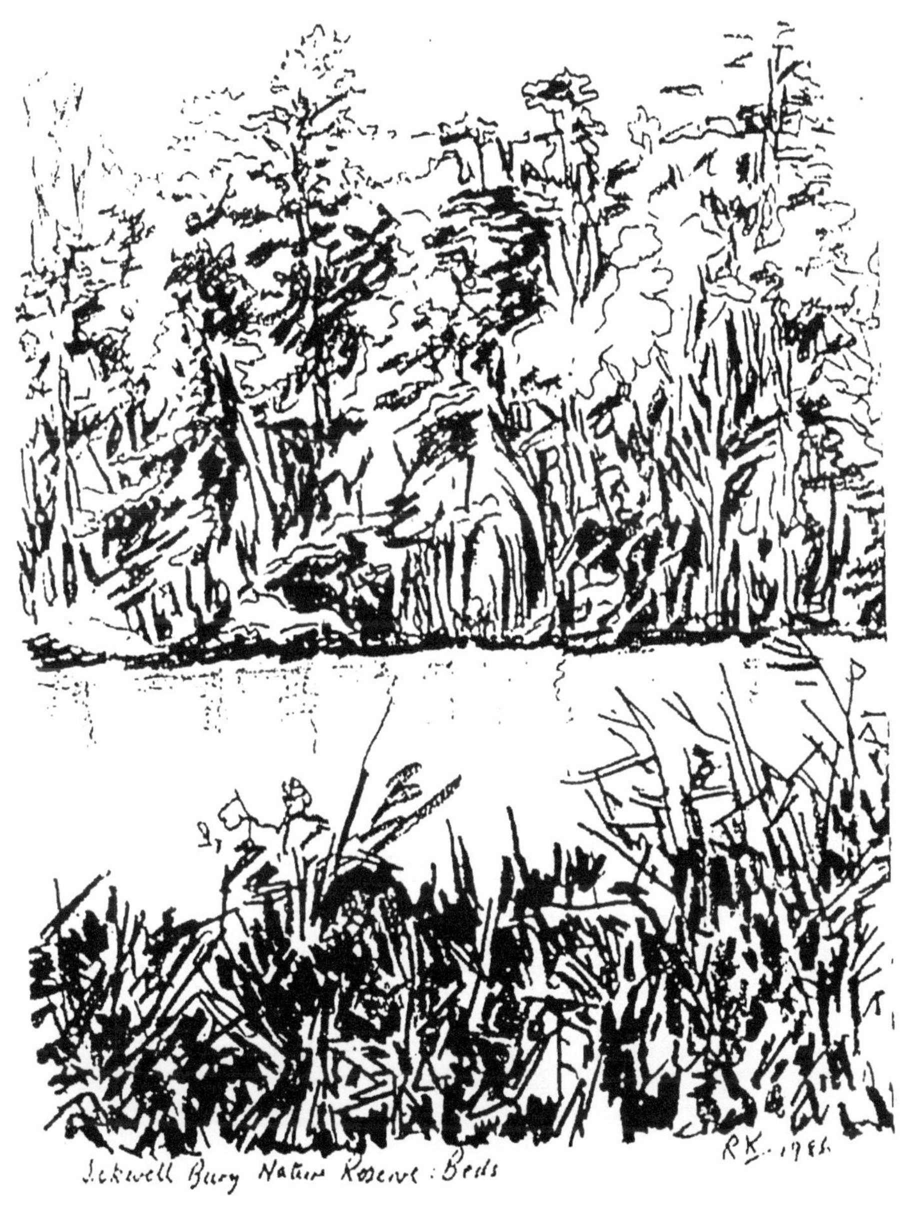

By leaving areas of the paper untouched, the nuances of tone are conveyed. Dramatic effect, contrast, mystery, perspective are achieved – as we draw we become a humble mediator between the subject, creative effort, observation, feelings, interpretation, and the finished drawing.

64

Let this cherry tree

Speak as priest or sage

To show that love and oneness

Is the goal we seek.

Parched Earth (Maldon Mud)

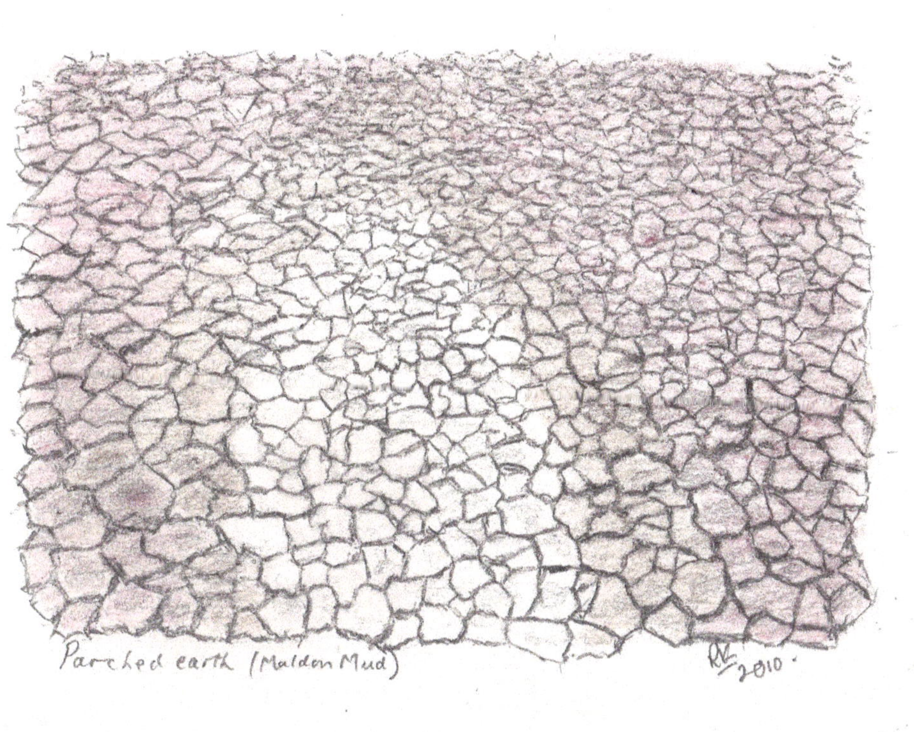

A hot day, certainly! Shining purple surfaces, reminiscent of water, upon the broken patches of mud, each drawn separately in order to maintain likeness and perspective. First attempt looked like scribble, (similar to taking a pencil for a walk across the paper as we did in primary school). Within this picture I find stillness, quiet, the 'here and now'.

65

Undemanding love

Allows us to speak

Of harmony within fate

This Winter solstice.

66

Moments of longing

Intrude much like fear

As if from another world

Concealed in my heart.

QE2 from Rainham Marshes

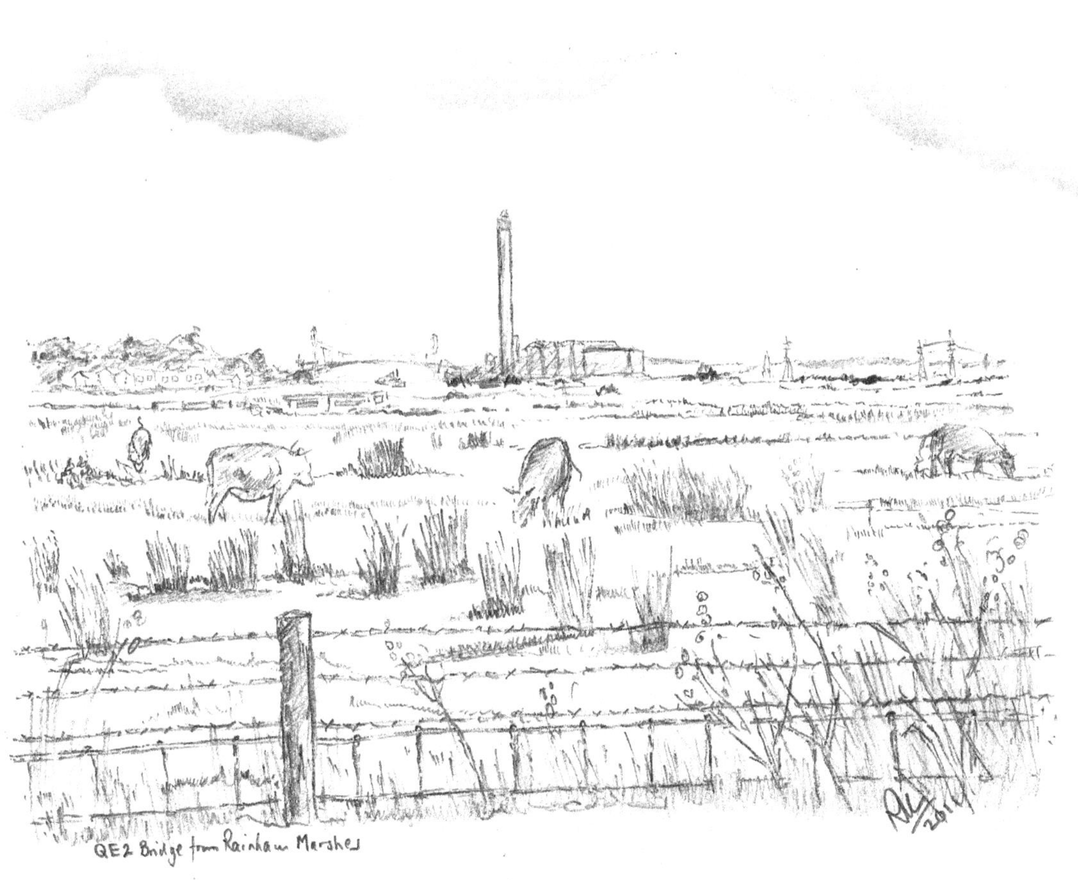

Flat, open, ancient marshland, and ditches (once a military firing range). Ship passing beneath the bridge, cows oblivious, completely in the present, land resisting urban expansion, behind the wire fence, leaving the scene to be itself, sensed rather than heard.

67

Winter shower drips

From the pointed roof

First suspended then falling

Like a love story.

68

Each day has a hue

Which forms and changes

Leaving our time to be seen

Only with hindsight.

From Westminster Bridge

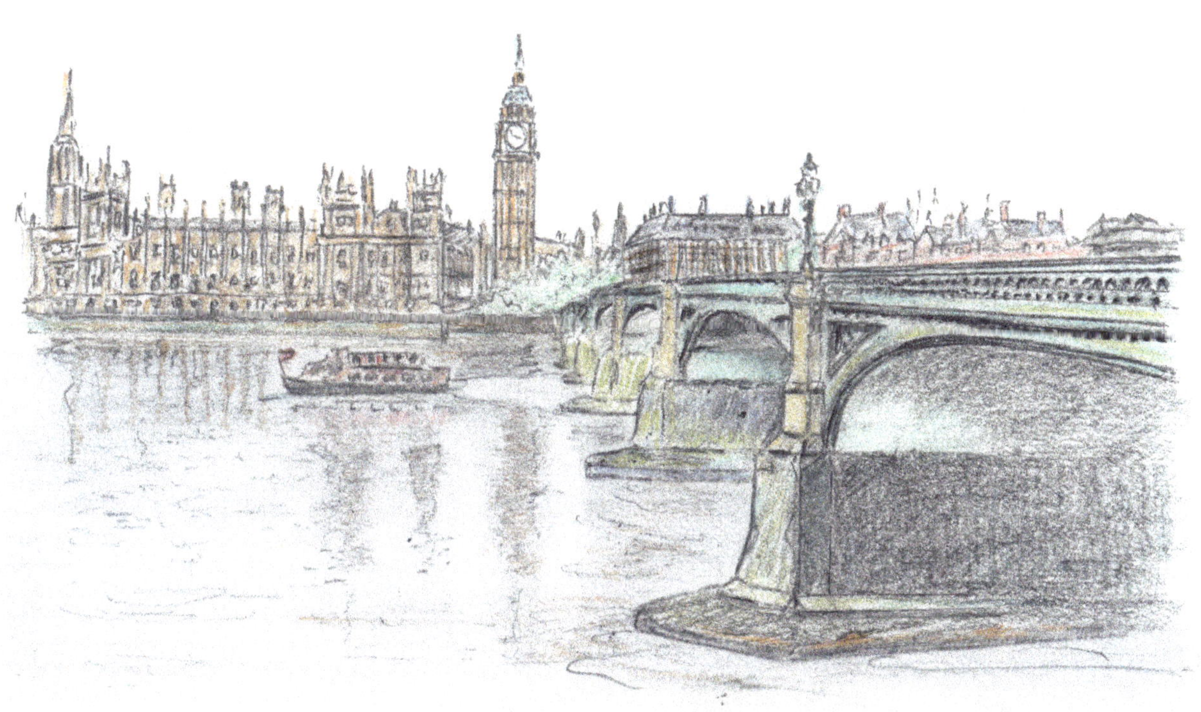

London. A grey morning, a personal vignette of a town where I once lived (and visit regularly) in a place where this connection is made, rich in life, emotion, meaning, submerged thoughts, feelings, and reflections.

69

Trick of light and shade

Brings various moods

The essential is not mine

As this life unfolds.

70

Frozen village pond

Stirs lost images

The past here in the present

As scenes remembered.

Marconi Tower, from Moulsham Mill

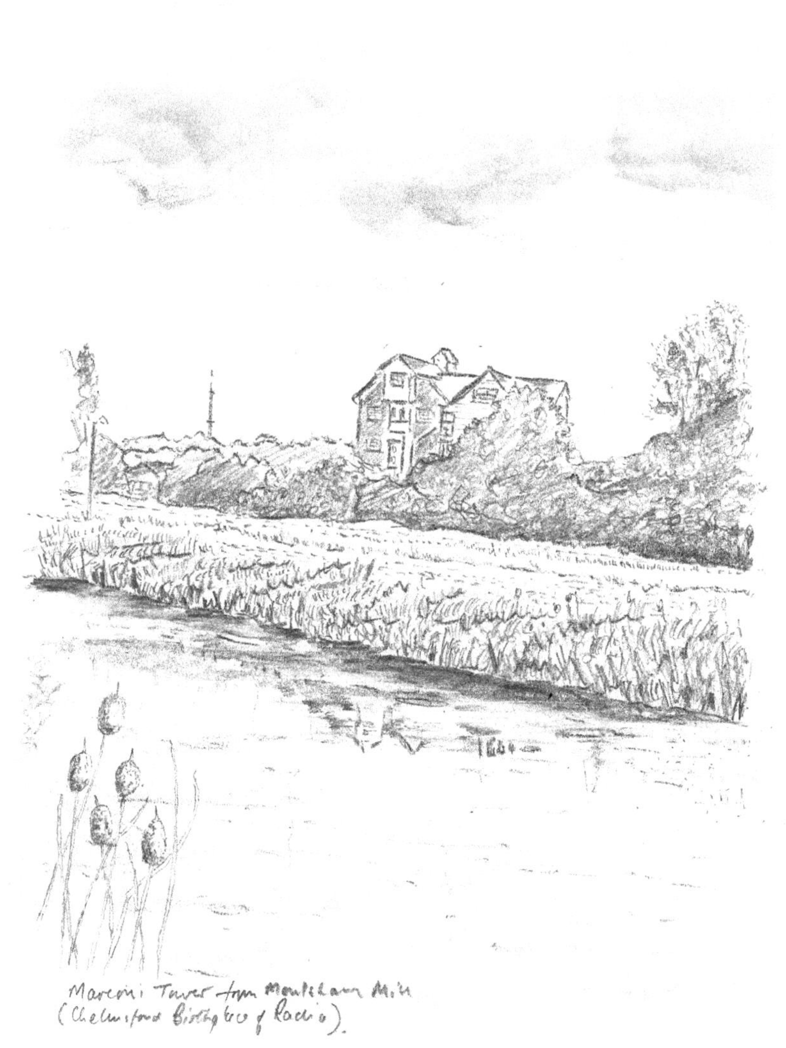

Chelmsford, the birthplace of radio. Marconi Tower in the distance, Bulrush in the foreground, tranquillity – an ephemeral motion that passes through us without containment, like a radio wave.

71

Stars rest patiently

In cobalt-blue sky

Young fingertips press against

The cold window pane.

For My Father

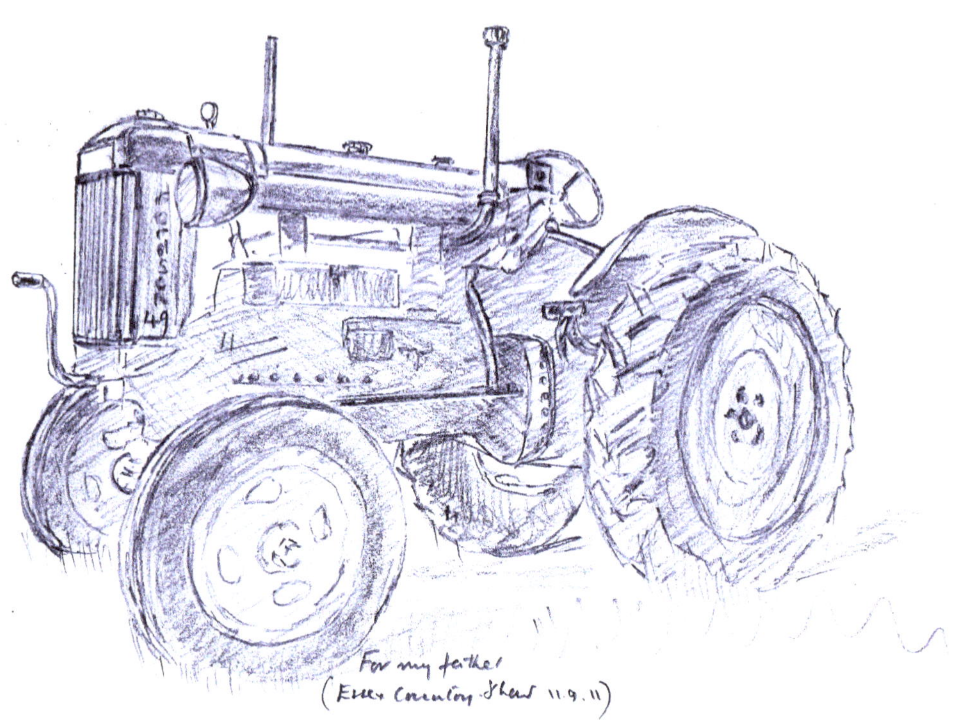

Seen as one of a collection of classic tractors, drawn in memory of my father (I remember, in the 1950s, seeing him drive a Fordson Major Tractor.) For me, I'm sure, a symbolic image, more than its obvious and immediate meaning. That unconscious aspect of our daily life and experience: perceptions, associations, projections, which lead us to select our chosen subjects, giving expression to the uniqueness of each of us.

Seed-drill

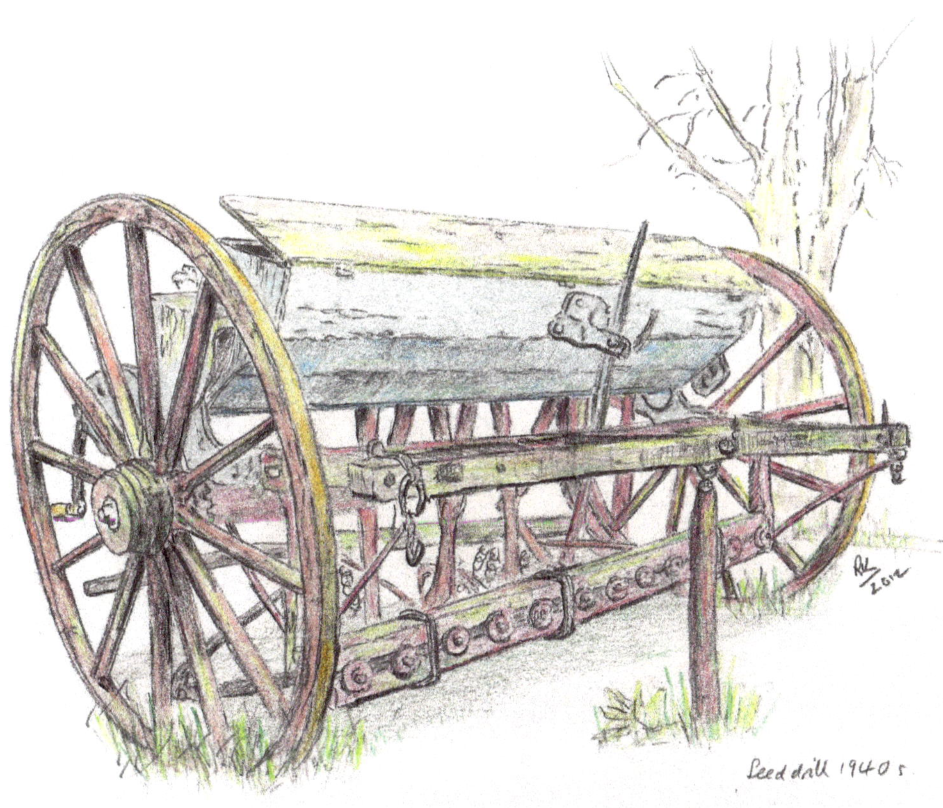

For centuries, the farmer, his family, and animals 'powered' the land... to be replaced in the twentieth century by machines. This drill still sits on the edge of an Essex field, its beautiful wheels no longer criss-crossing the landscape. Drawn, using coloured pencils, looking up towards this wonderful accomplishment, sowing seeds in evenly spaced rows, passion is recalled momentarily.

72

In accordance with

Being in oneness

There exists beyond touch, soul

Here in the tall grass.

Sitting in the Long Grass

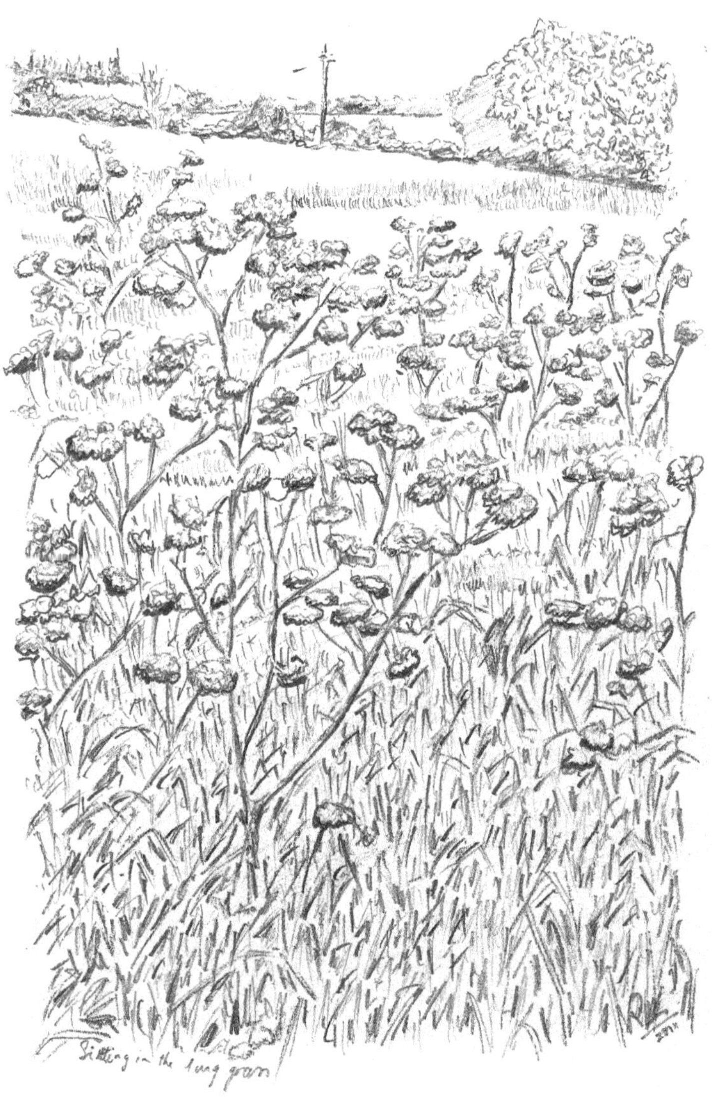

Sat upon the edge of a rut caused by a tractor and plough. Cow-parsley, almost the size of cauliflowers. Life and growth, the buzz of summertime. Discover the pleasure, the curiosity.

73

A gift of ripe plums

For a birthday tea

Born of the same God-essence

Like tomorrow's dew.

74

Watching the night fall

Upon the village

Silence was my companion

As thought fell to sleep.

From the Flood Plain

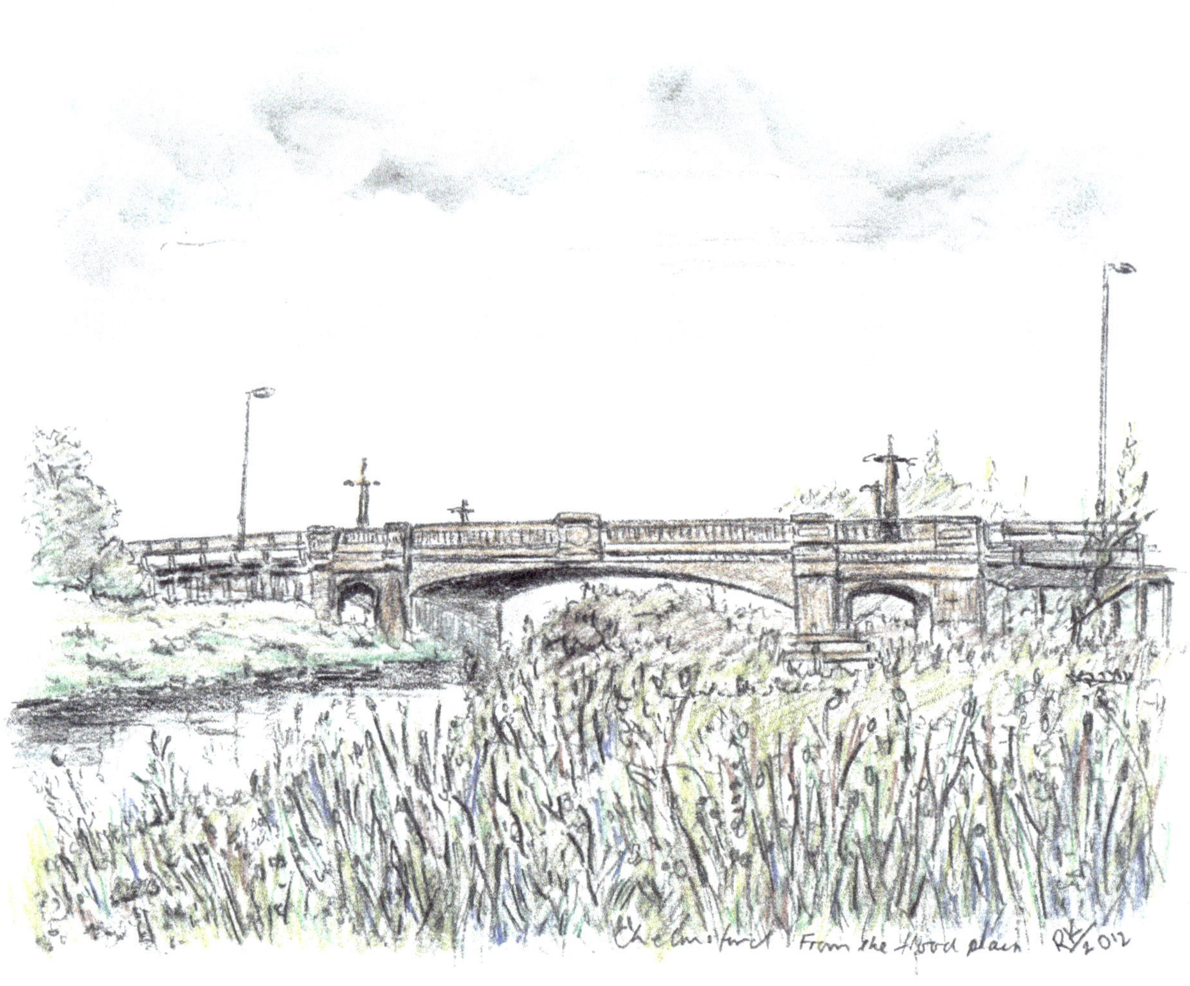

This bridge was built in 1938 in order to take traffic out of Chelmsford, to the new A12 by-pass. It spans across the flood plain. The landscape here reminds me of ages gone by, when Chelmsford was called Caesaromagus, of Saxon invasion, Danelaw and the Vikings, through to the Tudors, the Victorians, to the present day. Grazing cattle and horses, country fairs, ice skating on the frozen flood. The gas lamps on the bridge were never used, and now sit next to the towering, superior looking, electric replacements.

75

By the river's edge

Together we sat

Profound beyond all feeling

Nature's sweet music.

76

Everlasting grace

Was placed in my heart

An affirmation of life

Ennobled by love.

Footbridge (River Chelmer)

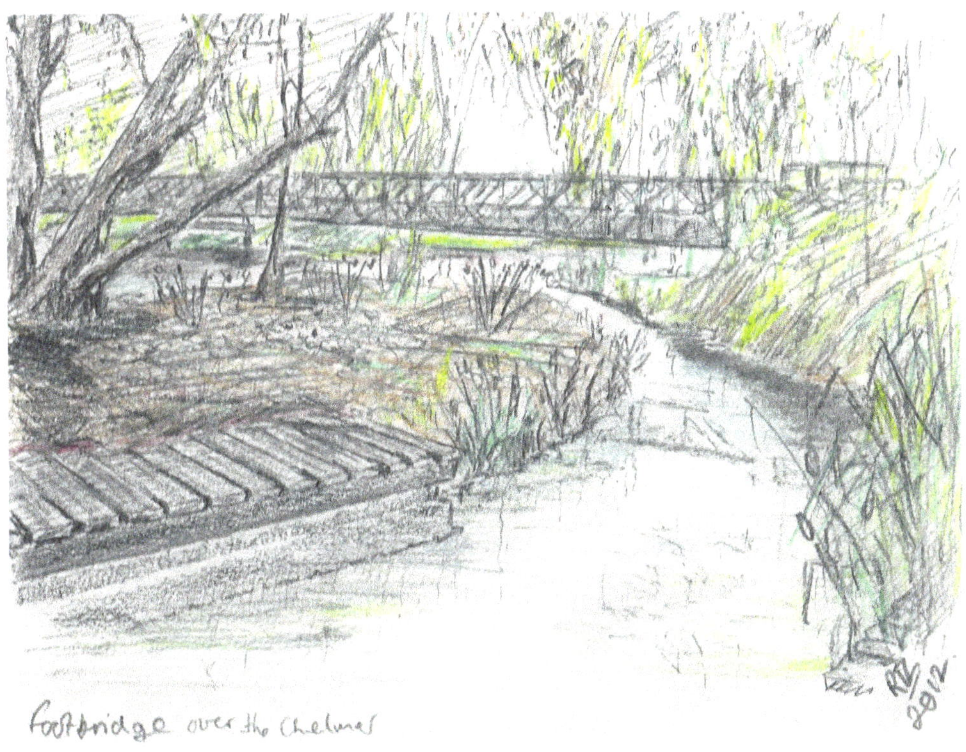

Quiet bend in the river. Combining pencil and colour, integrating the bridge with the trees and foliage. Soft reflections. This place once looked different, and will look different again.

77

Seated opposite

Aware of oneness

Integration of all life

Like sun-warmed air.

78

The unspoken word

Enshrined in my grip

I will always remember

As happening now.

Cambridgeshire Fens

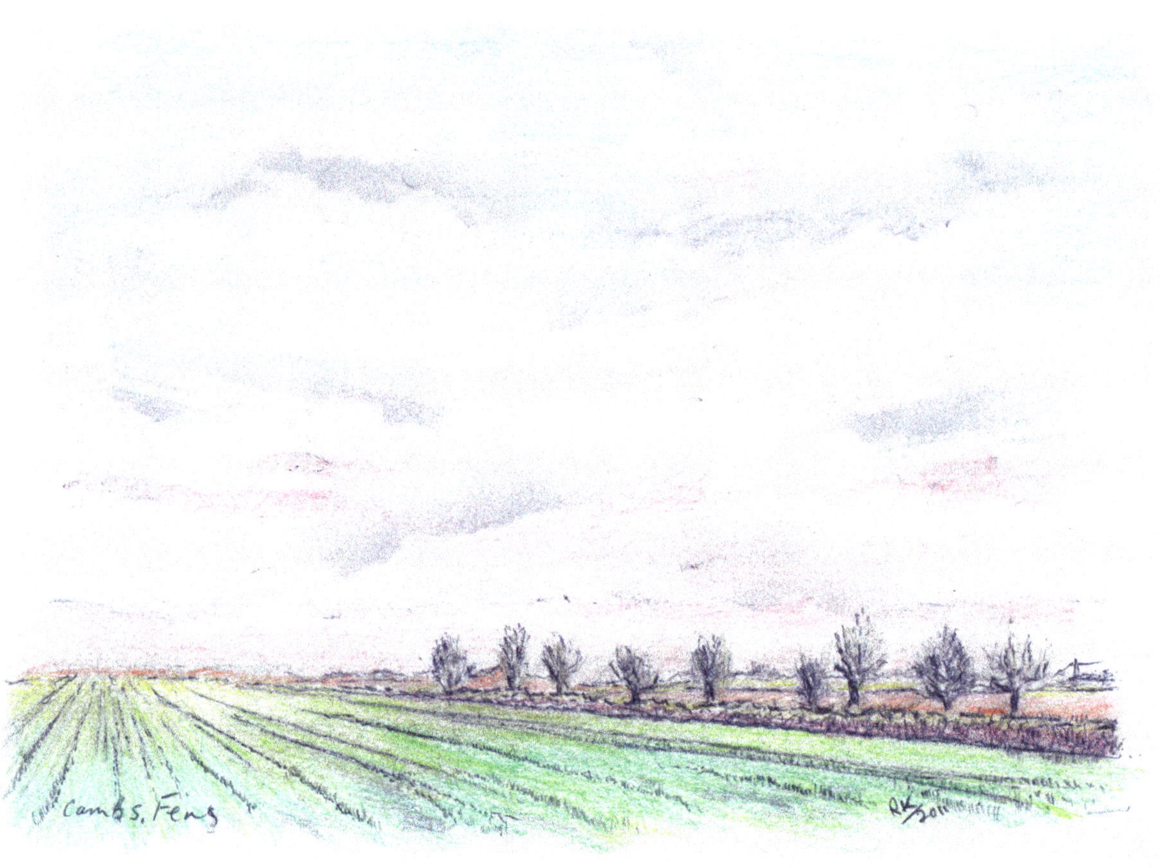

Fenland, in the morning, formed by nature, shaped by people over more than six thousand years. A naturally marshy region, drained over centuries, resulting in a flat, low-lying geography. Because of its cathedrals and churches, the Fens are sometimes called 'The Holy Land of England' – Ely Cathedral being a most unique example. Transfixed by sky and space, trying to take it all in, to be part of this landscape, just for a moment.

79

The bright sun departs

On a perfect day

Forget not your happiness

As the evening comes.

Pure Land, North Clifton, Notts

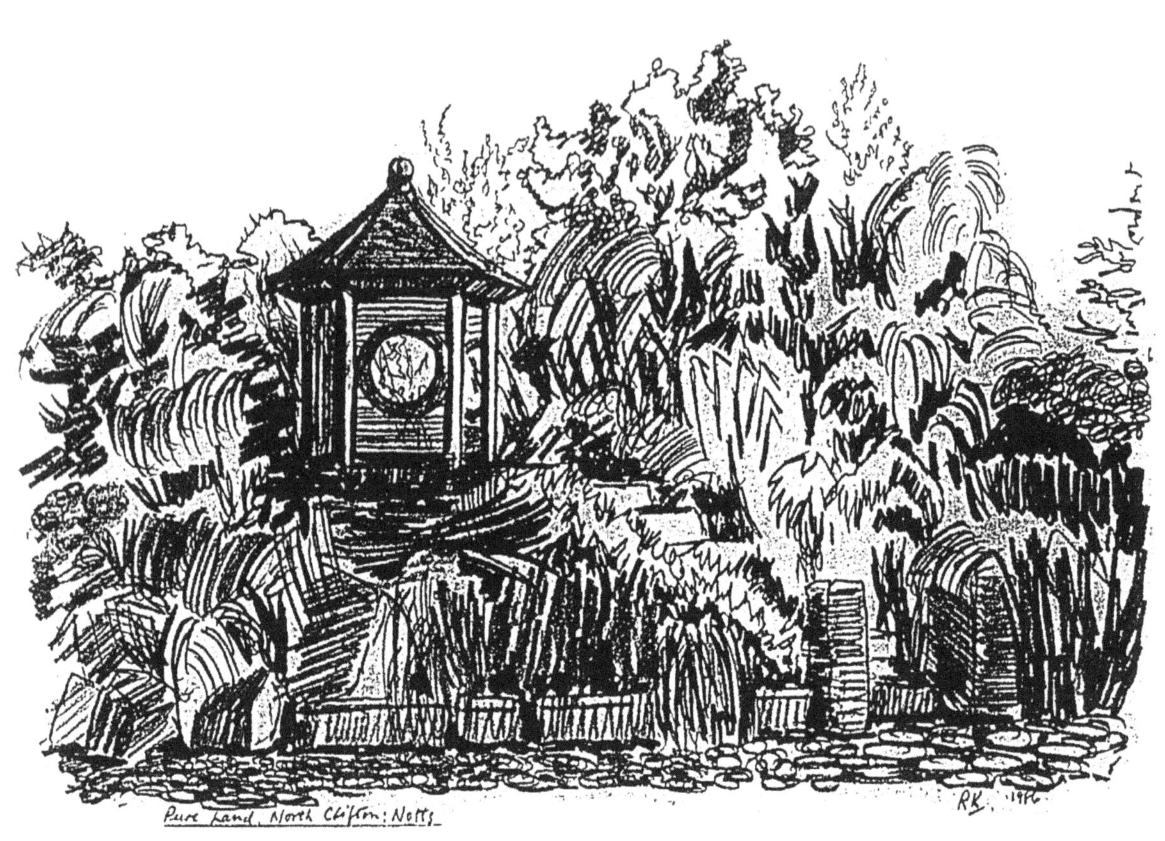

Spent many hours in this special place, with Buddha Matreya. Pure joy indeed, to be found, within this garden, within this creation.

Pottery

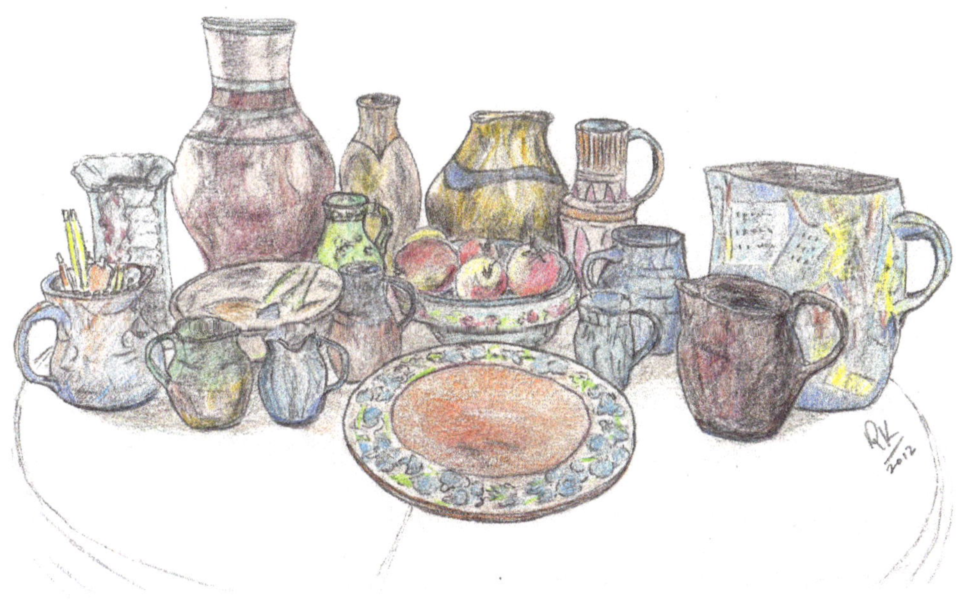

Examples of pottery made by Uncle Barney Lewis, in his retirement. Decorative, practical, a skill unearthed by him. Allegorical, story telling, hospitable. Still life drawing, as old as the Middle Ages, in this restless examination of life and nature.

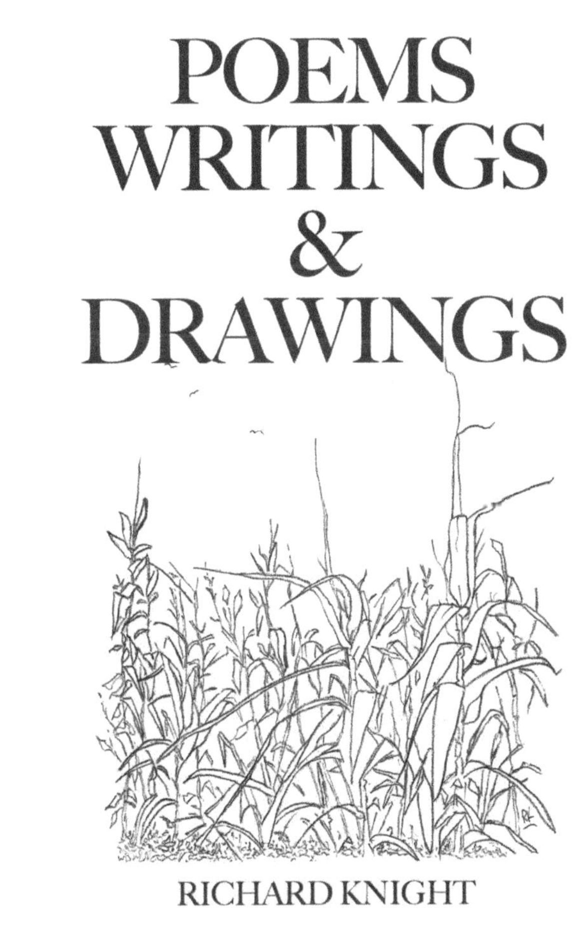

Volume One, also available from Amazon

www.ingramcontent.com/pod-product-compliance
Ingram Content Group UK Ltd.
Pitfield, Milton Keynes, MK11 3LW, UK
UKHW050136280726
14058UKWH00006B/677

9 780952 439257